Ingredients

Ingredients

by
Kim McCosker & Rachael Bermingham

4 Ingredients
PO Box 1171
Mooloolaba QLD 4557

ABN: 19 307 118 068

www.4ingredients.com.au
info@4ingredients.com.au

Cover & Logo Design: The Creative Collective www.thecreativecollection.com.au
Typesetting: BlueCrystal Creative; www.bluecrystalcreative.com
Printed in the UK by CPI Mackays, Chatham ME5 8TD

Distributor (World excluding USA): Simon & Schuster UK Ltd +44 (020) 7316 1900

ISBN: 978-0-85720-055-6

Introduction

Have you ever experienced any of the following?

1. *You look at your watch and you think 'Gosh, and it's 5:00 O'clock" what am I going to cook for dinner?*
2. *You collect your child from school and immediately they ask, "What's for dinner?"*
3. *You are DEFINITELY leaving work at 5:01pm and are still at your desk at 6:30pm...*
4. *You spend hours on the phone trying to explain how to cook something to your child who has just moved out?*
5. *OH MY GOD...They're coming for dinner!!!*
6. *Soccer practice goes longer than anticipated and you are just starting dinner at 6:00...*
7. *Go to the pantry look at it (full to the brim) and think "Nothing in there!"*
8. *Find yourself cooking spaghetti bolognaise for the kids AGAIN!!!*
9. *Spend all afternoon cooking and then have to clean what feels like a million things.*
10. *Have a hot date and want to impress and don't know where to start?*
11. *Groan and stress at the very thought of having to shop for 400 ingredients not to mention the big hole in the wallet afterwards?*
12. *Feel excited about cooking great food but without breaking the weekly food budget?*

And many other challenging culinary crises?

WELL THIS BOOK IS FOR YOU!

And your family, your friends
and their family and their friends....

What people are saying about 4 Ingredients

Hi Rachael and Kim, I purchased your book this week and all I can say is Thank you very much. I have 3 children, 8, 6 and 15 months and feeding the kids is difficult enough but I have a very fussy husband as well. He looked through your amazing book and told me about recipes he wanted to try, more so made with things he does not usually eat. Once again thanks for a new variety of meals that will be easier to prepare and a huge thank you from my bank account. **For the first time in the last 2 years I have been able to shop for our family for just under $250 a week. That was just amazing. My usual grocery bill comes in at $400.** Keep up the amazing work you are doing with helping to provide quick, easy and nutritious meals for my family. I'm certainly going to take this 'bible' with me to the next meeting of our school tuck shop. They will enjoy being able to give the kids more variety with a big green tick of approval. You are both legenda*ry.* *Thank you from Mandy Bryan and family*

Hi Rachael & Kim, Just by chance I noticed your Book 4 Ingredients 2, as I have sooooooo many cookbooks I felt I did not need another one, first the cover took my eye with 4 ingredients & the price was good, this afternoon I spent going through the book & I must say I am very impressed, as a 65 year old / modern woman I picked up so many quick yummy recipes & am looking forward to trying many out. **I used to cook for 70 people at our sons Ski Resort** down the Snowies & enjoyed the challenge of making fresh the choice of 2 Soups 2 main meals & 2 desserts I would have benefited then by having your easy recipes on hand. *Best Wishes. Kathleen Teal*

Hi Kim and Rachael, Saw your TV show on the Lifestyle channel, was so impressed by the simplicity and no-fuss approach, that I went out & bought your second book. My youngest child has developed into an **extremely fussy eater,** (even though we refuse to give in to her demands!), but each new recipe that I have put down in front of her, is now devoured with a "Yum!" response – the first time in years, as we normally have tears at the table each night! I am so impressed, that I have bought copies for my sister and friends in South Africa, including my dad, who is a widower, as he is struggling to cook for himself, but will enjoy the ease of your wonderful book! *Thank you, thank you, thank you and well done!! Jennifer Malcolm*

Hi Kim & Rachael, Congratulations on your book. I am a young [63] **retired chef** and my wife Nola now pleases me with her exquisite cooking skills. I admit that I was a sceptic of your " 4 Ingredients cook book" but it is now about 9.35 pm, and I have just got up from our dining room table after having one of the best salmon steak dinners ever [with a superb Pinot Grigio to accompany page 132 of your book [with no extras added] and I just had to send this email to you. Once again congratulations, I didn't think it possible. *Kind Regards Warren*

Hi there, I would like to congratulate you on stunning and wonderful recipe books. We moved to New Zealand from South Africa in May 2008. The first book caught my eye. I thought it was stunning and bought it on the spot. Today I went and bought the second book. I've just compiled a favourites list of all the recipes I use on a regular basis. **Within an hour of looking through the second book, I was back in store and bought the first and second books again - to send to a friend in South Africa.** I know she will love the books as I do. Once again thank you for the great books. It's like a bible in my kitchen having a 15 year old and 2 year old and both being too fussy too try anything new and different. *Kind regards Tanya E. Vivier*

Just wanted to say good job on the awesome cookbooks! My Mum recently bought me book 1 ... I loved it so much I went straight out and bought book 2! Recipes are so easy that even **my boyfriend doesn't have an excuse to buy takeaway now!** Thanks times a million and bring on the Gluten free 1. *Cheers, Tara Smithyman*

Hi Girls, I have just served your simple lemon cheesecake to my husband and son and am **an absolute hit!** (Well, actually, you girls are - I finally admitted to them after all the hmmmmms and aahhhhs and wows and groans of ecstasy that it was not my invention.) Wow - how simple and how tasty. My next try is your fruit cake as, being a diabetic, I am very conscious of what kind of treats I can have but also aware that my tastes and needs don't necessarily match theirs. Love your show and your recipes!! Keep it up.
Cheers and thanks. Lane Duck

I just love your books and wish they had been around when I was first married 54 years ago . Even now I am enjoying them so much have got rid of all my old cook books. life is so much easier and the food so beautiful and the hints fantastic. Loved your TV show too.
Thank you, Maureen

Foreword

Picture this ...

April 2006, two girlfriends were having a chat over a couple of red wines when Rachael presented Kim with a signed copy of her new book "Read My Lips!" Kim was admiring what her entrepreneurial friend had written when Rachael remarked "everyone has a good book inside them!" Kim quickly validated that statement by mentioning her own book idea "What is it?" Rach asked, "A book full of yummy recipes all made with 4 or fewer ingredients ..."

May 2006, together the busy Mums embark on the 4 Ingredient Journey. A plan was developed, a timeline set and tasks ticked off during their children's sleep times. Step 1 collect the recipes, step 2 cook them, step 3 write a book preparing quick, easy and delicious food by;

- **Reducing the number of ingredients required to make something yummy.** Our aim was to simplify without compromising on lavour!

- **Reduce the number of utensils required to make something yummy.** The only measuring utensils required to make the recipes in this book are a teaspoon, a tablespoon and a cup. Remaining measurements eg., millilitre (ml) or grams (g) can be purchased off the shelf in those quantities.

- **Reduce the amount of money spent on food each week.** Generally, a recipe with only 4 ingredients costs less to prepare than a recipe with 7, 8 or 9!

- **Create more time to spend doing what you love to do.** Saving time and money ... And who can't do with more of those these days?

November 2006, with our manuscript almost complete, excitement was mounting! We started to call publishers wondering which one would be the lucky one to gain our business and publish our sensational little book. After calling every publisher in Australia, we were STUNNED to discover that not one was interested in our book, in fact, some we couldn't even get past the secretary! "Are you famous?" they'd ask "No!" we'd reply and then they'd hang up!!!

December 2006, with no other option, we find ourselves self-publishing! We embark on a massive journey of refinancing a mortgage and printing the book ourselves ... Suddenly we are responsible for; editor, typesetter, designer, distributor and everything else that goes with getting a book from manuscript to completion.

March 14, 2007, (a date we'll never forget) 2,000 books arrive on our doorstep and we are off and running. To date this little venture has cost us $26,000! We were *hand delivering* books in order to generate cashflow to repay our homeloan. For 9 months (up till Christmas) we arrange and self fund hundreds of booksignings at hundreds of bookstores throughout Australia armed with plates of delicious taste tests from our book

December 2007, 4 Ingredients ends the year as the biggest selling book in Australia second only to Harry Potter and the Deathly Hallows! And is the number 1 selling book at that time in both Australia and New Zealand, we are exhausted but ELATED!!!!

February 2008 while 4 Ingredients comprised recipes we'd collected from family and friends, our second book 4 Ingredients 2 grew from recipes we collected from people we met at the vast amount of book signings and interviews we did where upon seeing our story people would generously jump onto our website and share their own 4 Ingredient recipe. We started to cook our way through another 1,000 recipes to select the best of the best to go into a new book.

March 2008, on the back of PHENOMENAL sales continuing we start filming our very own TV Show called ... 4 Ingredients!

September 1, 2008, finally after months of cooking, we launch 4 Ingredients 2.

Septmber 11, 2008, '4 Ingredients' the TV Show premiers.

September 30, 2008 4 Ingredients 2 is the biggest selling non-fiction title in Australia and New Zealand closely followed by 4 Ingredients. Collectively we have now printed over *1 MILLION* copies of our cookbooks (can you believe it!!!)

November 2008, we are on a plane to London to discuss the possibility of bringing our book to the UK ... Yep that's L.O.N.D.O.N!!!

TODAY, December 2008, ... 2 girls sit down to another couple glasses of red wine and take a moment to reflect ... HOOOLY MOOOLY – What a journey!

We are two average Mums who absolutely love and adore our families. We (like 80% of the world) are busy juggling a million things daily, trying to be the best Mum, wife, daughter, sister, friend etc that we possibly can be. We wrote a cookbook simply that we wanted to read..

How LUCKY are we that it has helped soooooo many others too! Men and women, young and old, now nearly 1 in 12 homes across Australia and New Zealand own a copy of our little book ... UNBELIEVEABLE!!!!!!!!!!!!!!!!!!!

And here we sit (both excited AND nervous), on the brink of launching into the UK market!!!!

To anyone out there who has ever thought, "What am I going to cook for dinner?" This book is for you and your family and your friends and their family and their friends!

BEST WISHES & HAPPY COOKING
KIM & RACHAEL

Kim   Rachael

www.4ingredients.co.uk

For more detailed information on how we wrote our book and how we made them the bestsellers they are, please visit our website www.4ingredients.com.au where you will find a book Rach has written about it.

In the cupboard

In 4 Ingredients 2 we have a suggestion of ingredients you may want to stock to help you create many a wonderful meals and treats from the pages within! *Please note: In this book we have not included salt, pepper & water as part of the 4 ingredients.*

Savoury	Sweet
Basil Pesto	Arrowroot biscuits
BBQ Sauce	Caster sugar
Beef & chicken stock cubes	Cinnamon
Breadcrumbs	Condensed milk
Cold pressed macadamia nut oil	Cornflour
Curry powder	Cream
Dijon mustard	Cream cheese
Extra virgin macadamia oil spray	Desiccated coconut
French onion soup (dry mix)	Eggs
Fresh vegetables	Evaporated milk
Garlic	Food colouring
Lemons	Fresh fruit
Minced ginger	Gelatine
Peppercorns	Honey
Pine nuts	Icing sugar
Rice	Jams: Apricot, strawberry
Sea salt	Jelly crystals
Sesame seeds	Marmalade
Shortcrust Pastry	Mixed fruit (homebrand)
Spaghetti & noodles	Mixed spices
Sour cream	Nutmeg
Soy sauce	Plain & self raising flour
Sweet chilli sauce	Pkt. bamboo skewers
Tinned soups: Asparagus, Celery etc.	Pkt. vanilla cake mix
Tomato sauce	Puff pastry (preferably with butter)
Whole-egg mayonnaise	Sugar (raw, brown)
Worcestershire sauce	Tinned fruit: Pineapple, pear
Vegetable Seasoning	Tin of pie apple
Vegetable Stock	Vanilla essence
Vinegar	

Guide to weights and measures

In an effort to make cooking easier we simplified our measuring system, all you need to make the recipes within 4 ingredients are;

- 1 Teaspoon = 1 tsp.
- 1 Tablespoon = 1 tbs.
- 1 Cup = **250ml** *or* the following;

	Grams per cup		Grams per cup
Almond meal	170	Nuts - Pecans	120
Butter	230	Nuts - Almonds	160
Basil Pesto	260	Nuts - Pistachios	120
Breadcrumbs	130	Pasta (dried)	75
Brown sugar, packed	220	Peanut butter	260
Caster sugar	200	Popcorn	40
Cheese	100	Raisins	170
Chutney	300	Rice	185
Cornflakes	120	Rice bubbles	80
Cornflour	120	Rolled oats	100
Desiccated coconut	120	Salsa	175
Dried apricots	160	Self raising flour	175
Dried mixed fruit	170	Sour cream	320
Flour	175	Sultanas	170
Honey	320	Sugar - White	220
Icing Sugar	120	Sugar - Raw	200
Jam	320	Tandoori paste	225
Mayonnaise	260	Tomato paste	260
Natural muesli	110	Yoghurt	250

Abbreviations used

- Gram   g
- Kilogram   kg
- Millilitre   ml
- Litre   ltr

Oven temperature guide

Making friends with your oven really helps when cooking. Basically the Celsius temperature is about half the Fahrenheit temperature.

A lot of ovens these days offer the option to bake or fan bake (amongst others), as a rule, having the fan assisted option on will greatly increase the temperature in your oven and will shorten cooking times.

Our recipes have been compiled assuming a conventional oven (fan-forced) unless otherwise stated. If however your oven is not fan forced as a general rule of thumb, conventional cooking temperatures are increased by 20C (this may vary between models). So if the recipe reads bake for 1 hour at 180C that will be 1 hour at 200C non fan-forced.

Here's some help:

	Fahrenheit	Celsius	Gas Mark
Slow	275	140	1
Slow	300	150	2
Mod	325	165	3
Mod	350	180	4
Mod hot	375	190	5
Mod hot	400	200	6
Hot	425	220	7
Hot	450	230	8
Very hot	475	240	9

Healthy Food Substitutes

What we would really have loved is to have substituted many of our everyday household products for healthier alternatives. The main reason being is that natural, non-technically enhanced products are *LOADED* with essential nutrients that fuel your body, mind and soul. Apart form the obvious short and long term benefits of consuming these ingredients, you can literally taste the difference.

However not wanting to isolate those that are not able to purchase these products readily, we did not include these within our recipes, opting instead to add this section, which we feel, is vital to your and your families' health. For those of you able to access these products readily the table below will show you what mainstream ingredient can be easily substituted with a healthier (and less technically altered and therefore nutrient drained) alternative. For more information on this we recommend our good friend Cyndi O'Meara's book; Changing Habits Changing Lives:

Product	Substitute
Sugar	• Organic Raw Sugar*
Oil	• Cold pressed Extra Virgin Olive Oil*
	• Cold Pressed Macadamia Nut Oil*
Spray Oil	• Cold Pressed Macadamia Nut Oil *
Flour	• Spelt Flour
	• Organic Plain Flour & Organic Baking Powder*
	• Organic Self Raising Flour
Margarine	• Butter*
Eggs	• Organic Free-range Eggs*
Milk	• Organic Milk*
	• Raw Milk (pasteurised only milk)
Pasta	• Made from fresh ingredients
	• Organic Pasta*
Honey	• Manuka Honey*
	• Organic Honey*
Jams	• Organic Jam*
	• Homemade Jams made from raw ingredients
Soy Sauce	• Tamari Soy Sauce*

Note – all ingredients with an asterisk * can now be bought in your local supermarket.

Table of Contents

Breakfasts

Eat breakfast like a king, lunch like a prince and dinner like a pauper

Adelle Davis

Almond Muffins

Makes 12

- *2 cups (340g) almond meal*
- *2 tsp. baking powder*
- *½ cup (115g) butter, melted*
- *4 eggs*

Preheat oven to 160C. Grease a non-stick muffin tin well with butter. Mix dry ingredients together plus ¼ tsp. salt. Add wet ingredients plus ⅓ cup water and mix thoroughly, distribute evenly into muffin trays and bake for 15 - 18 minutes.

Optional: Add 1 cup fresh blueberries or raspberries to the mix.

Bacon & Egg Muffin

Makes 1. A recipe from Brett McCosker

- *1 English muffin*
- *1 egg*
- *1 rasher of bacon*
- *1 tbs. BBQ Sauce*

Fry your egg and bacon, place on absorbent paper. Toast muffin in a toaster, spread with BBQ sauce and top with bacon and egg.

Optional: Add a slice of cheese.

Bircher Muesli

Serves 1

- ½ cup (110g) natural muesli
- ¼ cup (75ml) orange juice
- 2 tbs. natural yoghurt
- 1 green apple, grated

Soak the muesli in the juice for 15 minutes. Mix in remaining ingredients and serve ... YUMMY!

Chestnut Topping

Serves 2

- 3 tbs. butter
- 1 tbs. brown sugar
- 125g cooked, peeled chestnuts

Finely chop the chestnuts. Melt the butter in a small fry pan. Add the brown sugar and stir until dissolved. Add the chestnuts and saute until just browned.

Tip: A delicious topping on pancakes.

Citrus Pancakes

Makes 4. Our children love these.

- *1 cup (175g) self raising flour*
- *1 egg*
- *1 cup (250ml) milk*
- *1 orange, finely grate the peel from the whole orange*

Sift flour, add egg and a pinch of salt. Beat gradually adding milk until thick and smooth. Add orange zest. Heat a non-stick frying pan. Pour desired quantity into frying pan, cook until bubbling on top and then flip.

Optional: Serve with maple syrup, lemon juice and sugar, honey or stewed fruits.

Crumpets with Strawberries

Serves 2

- *4 crumpets*
- *2 tbs. honey*
- *8 strawberries washed, hulled and sliced*
- *200g tub mocha flavoured yoghurt*

Toast crumpets then drizzle evenly with honey. Top with strawberries and yoghurt.

Optional: Substitute mocha yoghurt for yoghurt of choice.

Damper

Serves 2. Thanks for the idea, Jeremy Horwood.

- *2 cups (350g) self raising flour*
- *1½ cups (375ml) milk*
- *1 tsp. sugar*
- *1 tsp. butter*

Sift the flour and sugar into a bowl and add a pinch of salt. Add butter and enough milk to make a manageable dough. Shape into a flat ball and place on a greased and floured oven tray, bake at 220C for 25 - 30 minutes, baste with milk during cooking.

Optional: Serve hot with lashings of butter and golden syrup or jam.

English Muffin with Strawberries

Serves 1. This is a really lovely way to start the day!

- *1 English muffin*
- *2 tsp. cream cheese*
- *6 fresh strawberries, washed, hulled and quartered*
- *2 tbs. maple syrup*

Cut muffin in half and toast. Spread cream cheese on both muffins, top with strawberries and drizzle with maple syrup.

Fluffy Cheese Omelette

Makes 2

- *3 eggs*
- *½ cup (50g) grated cheese*
- *1 tbs. butter*

Beat whites of eggs stiffly with pinch of salt. Lightly fold in yolks and 3 tbs. cold water, then grated cheese. Melt butter in a pan and over medium heat pour in mixture. Cook till golden brown underneath. Brown top under griller or turn with egg flipper.

Grilled Apple, Banana & Ricotta Stack

Makes 1. This is a charming breakfast, your guests will be impressed!

- *1 apple*
- *1 banana*
- *2 tbs. fresh ricotta*
- *1 tbs. honey*

Slice and grill the apple for 3 minutes. Layer apple and banana. Top with ricotta and drizzle honey over all.

Optional: This is also delicious done with pear rather than apple, or a combination of both.

Grilled Grapefruit

Makes 2

- *2 medium grapefruit (ask for a sweeter variety)*
- *1 tbs. honey*
- *1 tbs. brown sugar*
- *200g tub vanilla yoghurt*

Halve grapefruits and carefully loosen pulp with a sharp knife. Combine honey and brown sugar. Place grapefruit in a small ovenproof dish and drizzle with the honey/sugar mixture. Place under preheated grill for 3 - 4 minutes or until lightly browned. Serve with yoghurt.

Grilled Pears with Yoghurt

Makes 2

- *2 pears*
- *4 tbs. yoghurt (flavour of your choice)*

Slice and grill pears for 3 minutes. Top with yoghurt.

Healthy Breakfast on the go

Serves 4

- *200g tub fruit yoghurt*
- *1 free-range egg*
- *200g watermelon, diced*
- *2 bananas, diced (or fruit of choice, strawberries, pineapple, apples)*

Place all ingredients into a blender and serve. A fantastic breakfast to take with you.

Praline Toast

Serves 4

- *6 slices bread*
- *¼ cup (55g) butter, softened*
- *¼ cup (25g) pecans, finely chopped*
- *½ cup (110g) brown sugar*

Mix together butter, pecans and sugar then spread it on bread slices. Place in preheated 180C oven and bake until brown and bubbly.

Waffle, Strawberries & Yoghurt

Serves 4

- *8 Belgian waffles*
- *1 punnet strawberries, washed, hulled and quartered*
- *200g tub vanilla yoghurt*

Lightly toast the waffles. Fold half the strawberries through the yoghurt and pour over the waffles. Top with remaining strawberries.

Scrambled Eggs

Serves 4

- *4 eggs, beaten*
- *¼ cup (125ml) milk*
- *¼ cup (65g) cottage cheese*
- *1 tbs. extra virgin olive oil*

Beat eggs together in a small bowl. Add milk and season with salt and pepper, add cottage cheese and stir. Pour oil in a large frying pan, when warm add the egg mixture. Let cook until the mixture starts to bubble. Use a spatula to lift and mix until well cooked. Take care not to burn the cottage cheese.

Wholemeal Damper

Serves 6

- *500g wholemeal self raising flour*
- *4 tsp. baking powder*
- *2½ cups (625ml) milk*
- *2 tbs. golden syrup*

Preheat oven to 180C. Together with a teaspoon of salt, combine all ingredients. Knead lightly and shape into a high, round bun. Bake for 30 minutes.

Optional: Serve with lashings of butter and golden syrup!

Zucchini Fritters

Serves 2

- *2 eggs*
- *¼ red onion, grated*
- *½ zucchini, grated*
- *2 tbs. grated carrot*

Beat eggs and add remaining ingredients, season for taste. Heat a small non-stick frying pan over medium heat. Spoon 2 x 2 tbs. of mixture into the pan, leaving room for spreading. Cook for 2 minutes each side.

Dips, Salad Dressings & Sauces

There is more hunger for love and appreciation in this world than for bread

Mother Teresa

Avocado Salsa

A recipe from Michelle Dodd.

- *1 large ripe avocado*
- *½ vine ripened tomato, diced*
- *½ red onion, finely chopped*
- *3 tbs. chopped coriander*

Mash avocado (reserving seed), add remaining ingredients and mix well. Place the seed back into the dip to help prevent discolouration and refrigerate until needed.

Corn Relish Dip

Makes 1 cup

- *125g cream cheese, softened*
- *125g sweet corn relish*

Beat cheese until smooth, add corn relish and combine. Serve with fresh vege sticks or yummy crackers.

Crab Dip

Recipe from Cyndi O'Meara.

- *250g cream cheese, softened*
- *¾ cup (185ml) sweet chilli sauce*
- *170g tin crabmeat, drained*

Spread Cream cheese on a small platter, cover with chilli sauce and sprinkle with crabmeat.

French Onion Dip

- *320ml sour cream*
- *⅓ pkt French onion soup (may need a little more)*

Mix soup into sour cream and chill before serving. Serve with fresh celery and carrot sticks.

Garlic Avocado Dip

- *2 large, ripe avocados*
- *2 large cloves fresh garlic*
- *1 tsp. sea salt*
- *1 lemon*

Mash avocado, reserving seed. Place salt and garlic into a mortar and pound until well combined. Place avocado and garlic salt mix into a food processor together with the juice of ½ a lemon. Blend well and check seasoning. Place the seed back into the dip to help prevent discolouration and refrigerate until needed.

Grilled Cheese Salsa Dip

A Mexicana marvel ... Too easy and too tasty!

- *250g edam or gouda*
- *2 tbs. cream*
- *½ cup (125g) salsa*

Shred cheese, place in small saucepan. Cook on low-medium stovetop, let cheese melt then add cream, stirring frequently to make sure cheese doesn't scorch the dish. Transfer to a warm dish, top with salsa.

Optional: Serve with fresh raw vegetables and corn chips ... mmmm!

Holy Guacamole

A recipe from the very generous Yvonne Ormsby

- *3 avocados*
- *½ cup (125g) salsa*
- *¼ cup (80ml) sour cream*
- *1 pkt corn chips*

Mash avocados, add salsa, sour cream and a pinch of sea salt and mix well. Serve with corn chips.

Hummus

A recipe by Michelle Dodd.

- *300g can chickpeas, drain*
- *1 garlic clove, crushed*
- *2 tbs. lemon juice*
- *1 tbs. tahini*

Blend all ingredients in a food processor.

Optional: Serve with fresh vegetables and crackers.

Paprika Dip

- *200g creme fraiche*
- *1 tsp. smoked paprika*

Mix the two ingredients together. Chill before serving with a plate full of fresh vegetable sticks.

Raita

Makes 1 cup

- *½ an onion*
- *1 tbs. fresh mint*
- *1 tbs. coriander*
- *200ml natural yoghurt*

Finely chop the onion, mint, coriander and mix together in a bowl with yoghurt.

Ricotta & Chutney Dip

- 250g ricotta cheese
- ½ cup (150g) of mango chutney (any fruit chutney is nice)
- ¼ cup (30g) mixed nuts, chopped
- 1 pkt pappadums

Mix ricotta and chutney until well combined then add nuts. Serve with pappadums.

Smoked Salmon Dip

- 300g pkt smoked salmon, finely chopped
- 2 tbs. cream
- 1 tsp. horseradish cream
- 1 tsp. chopped chives

Combine all and mix well.

Optional: Pile onto thick slices of Lebanese cucumber or Lebanese bread.

Salad Dressings

What you focus on most you attract, so make each thought count towards your betterment rather than your detriment

Rachael Bermingham

Balsamic & Garlic Dressing

- *2 tbs. balsamic vinegar*
- *¼ cup (60ml) lemon juice*
- *1 clove garlic, crushed*
- *¾ cup (185ml) olive oil*

Combine all ingredients in a screw top jar and shake well.

Classic Salad Dressing

- *½ cup (125ml) freshly squeezed lemon juice*
- *4 tbs. extra virgin olive oil*
- *2 tsp. Dijon mustard*
- *2 cloves garlic, crushed*

Place all ingredients in a screw top jar, season with sea salt and pepper and shake well.

Optional: This is divine served over the Basil & Lentil Salad (see Salads).

Cocktail Sauce

- ½ cup (130g) mayonnaise
- ½ cup (125ml) tomato sauce
- ½ tsp. Worcestershire sauce
- 2 tbs. cream

Combine all ingredients in a bowl, season with sea salt and pepper and stir well.

Creamy Salad Dressing

This is absolutely *SENSATIONAL*, will make a salad eater of anyone!!!

- ⅔ part natural Greek yoghurt
- ⅓ part whole egg mayonnaise

Mix well and serve over salad.

Easy Thai Dressing

- 2 tbs. sugar
- 2 tbs. lime juice
- ⅓ cup (80ml) fish sauce
- Chilli powder to taste

Combine all ingredients in a screw top jar and shake well.

Honey Mustard Dressing

- *2 tsp. honey*
- *1½ tbs. Dijon mustard*
- *2 tbs. white wine vinegar*
- *½ cup (125ml) extra virgin olive oil*

Place honey and mustard in a small bowl, season with sea salt and pepper. Add vinegar and stir with a fork until completely dissolved. Slowly add oil while whisking vigorously. Taste and adjust seasonings if necessary.

Potato Salad Dressing

A recipe from the very talented Verna Day.

- *125g cream cheese*
- *⅔ cup (210g) sour cream*
- *1 tbs. chopped mint*
- *1 tbs. sweet chilli sauce*

Combine all with an electric mixer and pour over potatoes (enough for 6 potatoes).

Spinach & Strawberry Salad Dressing

- ⅓ cup (80ml) balsamic vinegar
- ⅔ cup (165ml) extra virgin olive oil
- 2 tsp. caster sugar
- 1 tbs. finely chopped fresh chives

Combine all ingredients in a jar, adding 1 tbs. of water and salt and pepper to taste. Shake really, really well. Taste and adjust seasonings, if required.

Optional: Delicious served over the Spinach and Strawberry Salad (see Salads).

Tomato Chutney Dressing

- ½ cup (130g) mayonnaise
- 2 tbs. tomato chutney
- 1 tbs. Dijon mustard

Mix ingredients together until combined. Serve with grilled fish.

Vinaigrette

- ½ cup (125ml) olive oil
- ½ cup (125ml) white wine vinegar
- 4 - 6 sprigs flat-leaf parsley, finely chopped
- 2 tsp. Dijon mustard

Combine all ingredients in a screw-top jar and shake well.

Wasabi Dressing

A recipe by Tanya Ormsby.

- *2 tsp. wasabi*
- *⅓ cup (80ml) lemon juice*
- *⅓ cup (80ml) peanut oil*
- *2 tsp. finely chopped fresh dill*

Combine all ingredients in a screw top jar and shake well.

Sauces

An eye for an eye leaves the whole world blind

Gandhi

Barbequed Stir Fry Sauce

- ½ cup (125ml) BBQ Sauce
- 2 tsp. minced ginger
- 2 tbs. soy sauce

Simply mix. Delicious in a beef stir fry.

Beer Batter

A recipe from Rach's brother Anthony 'Spud' Moore.

- 1 cup (250ml) beer
- 1 cup plain flour
- 2 egg whites

Whisk egg whites until light and fluffy. Place flour and a pinch of sea salt in a bowl, mix in beer until smooth and lump free. Fold in egg whites and allow to stand for 10 - 15 minutes before using.

Best 'In-a-hurry' Sauce

Serve with any meat and Asian steamed vegetables.

* *1 clove garlic, crushed*
* *¼ cup (60ml) sweet chilli sauce*
* *¼ cup (60ml) soy sauce*
* *2 tsp. freshly grated ginger*

Combine all ingredients and mix well.

Caramel Sauce

This is heaven served over just about anything!

* *250ml cream*
* *¾ cup (165g) brown sugar*
* *¾ cup (170g) unsalted butter*

Combine all ingredients in a small saucepan and bring to the boil over medium heat. Simmer for 2 minutes.

Chilli Mayonnaise

* *½ tsp. sambal oelek*
* *⅓ cup (75g) whole egg mayonnaise*
* *¼ tsp. ground cumin*
* *2 tbs. sour cream*

Combine all ingredients in a bowl, mix well for a delicious flavour.

Optional: Add 1 tbs. freshly chopped coriander. Delicious served with sweet potato chips (see Potato section).

Easy Mocha Sauce

- *220g dark chocolate*
- *300ml cream*
- *2 tsp. instant coffee*

Place chocolate in a microwave safe dish and melt, stirring every 20 seconds until nice and smooth. Add cream and coffee and mix. Serve with Poached Pears (see Desserts) – simply stunning!

Easy Satay

- *½ cup (130g) crunchy peanut butter*
- *2 tbs. sweet chilli sauce*
- *¾ cup (185ml) liquid vegetable stock*
- *1 tbs. freshly chopped coriander*

Combine peanut butter, sweet chilli sauce and stock, cook stirring continually for 2 - 3 minutes. Serve in dipping plate topped with fresh coriander.

Optional: Delicious served with wedges and mezze of fresh vegetables (cucumber, carrot, celery, cherry tomatoes, etc).

Garlic Butter

- *¼ cup (55g) soft butter*
- *2 cloves garlic, crushed*
- *1 tsp. lemon juice*
- *¼ tsp. finely chopped parsley*

Mix all together and season with sea salt and pepper.

Optional: Slice a French stick every 3cm and spread the garlic butter generously, cover with foil and bake at 180C for 10 minutes.

Ginger & Mango Sauce

- *425g mangoes in juice*
- *1 pkt French onion soup mix*
- *1 tbs. minced ginger*

Puree mangoes and juice in a food processor or blender. Add onion soup mix and ginger and mix thoroughly. Pour into saucepan. Bring to boil and simmer for 5 minutes. Yummy served with meat and chicken.

Tip: Use fresh mango in season.

Honey Soy Garlic Marinade

Makes 1 cup.

- *10 tbs. honey*
- *Juice from 1 lemon*
- *6 tbs. soy sauce*
- *4 cloves of garlic, crushed*

Mix all ingredients together and smear onto meat allowing to marinate for at least 2 hours before grilling.

Optional: This is lovely on poultry and pork.

Horseradish Cream

This is yummy served with roast beef or corned beef.

- *½ cup (160g) sour cream*
- *2 tbs. horseradish cream*
- *2 tsp. chopped spring onions*
- *1 tsp. white balsamic or white wine vinegar*

Combine sour cream, horseradish cream, spring onions and vinegar in small bowl. Heat over low heat if serving with warm meat.

Horseradish, Mustard & Walnut Cream Sauce

- *1 cup (320g) sour cream*
- *1 tbs. Dijon mustard*
- *¼ cup (65g) horseradish cream*
- *½ cup (60g) roasted walnuts, finely chopped*

Mix all ingredients well. Lovely served with fish or chicken.

Mango Salsa

- *1 mango, cubed*
- *1 lime*
- *½ red finger chilli*
- *3 stems of fresh coriander, finely chopped*

Cut the lime in half, juice and zest one half. Cut chilli in half, remove the seeds and chop very finely. Combine all ingredients adding sea salt and pepper to taste. Serve with grilled fish or prawns.

Mixed Berry Sauce

- ½ cup (125ml) cream
- ¼ cup (55g) brown sugar
- 220g frozen mixed berries

Heat cream and sugar, stirring until sugar dissolves. Add mixed berries and cook, stirring for 2 minutes. Cool before spooning over vanilla ice-cream or basic cheesecake.

Onion Jam

- 3 large Spanish onions
- 3 tbs. balsamic vinegar
- ½ cup (110g) brown sugar
- 2 tbs. extra virgin olive oil

Slice onion into thin strips. Add onion to a preheated pot and cook until completely collapsed. Add vinegar and sugar and stir, turn pot down to a low heat. Leave on low heat until a jam-like consistency, stirring occasionally.

Optional: This is a great topper over steak or sausages.

Pesto Pleasure

- ½ cup (160g) sour cream
- ¼ cup (65g) basil pesto

Mix together. Serve with pasta, potatoes or steamed green vegetables such as asparagus or broccoli.

Soy & Ginger Dipping Sauce

- *⅓ cup (80ml) soy sauce*
- *2 tsp. white sugar*
- *1 - 2 cm piece ginger, grated*

Combine all in a small saucepan, stir over low heat until the sugar dissolves.

Optional: This is d.e.l.i.c.i.o.u.s served with honey and orange prawns (see Cocktail Food section).

Tempura Batter

- *⅔ cup (120g) plain flour*
- *⅓ cup (40g) cornflour*
- *¾ can very cold soda water*

Sift flour in a bowl and add a pinch of sea salt. Make a well in the center and add soda water, mix well until smooth and lump free. Set aside for 10 - 15 minutes before using.

Optional: Use small cut vegetables and meats and shallow fry.

White Sauce

- *2 tbs. butter*
- *2 tbs. flour*
- *1 cup (250ml) milk*

Melt butter in saucepan and remove from heat. Stir in flour and blend in milk. Return to heat, stir until sauce boils and thickens, and simmer for 2 minutes. Season with sea salt and pepper and add extra milk if required.

Yoghurt Dipping Sauce

A lovely healthy accompaniment to any Indian flavoured dish.

- *200g tub natural yoghurt*
- *1 medium cucumber*
- *2 tbs. lemon juice*
- *1 tbs. chopped mint leaves*

Combine all in a serving bowl.

Cocktail Food

Every person is a new door to a different world

From the movie Six Degrees of Separation

thanks to Steve's Famous Quotes

Asparagus Canapés

A recipe from Wendy Beattie, like the lady …Absolutely Fabulous!

- *2 bunches asparagus*
- *125g camembert cheese*
- *100g prosciutto*

Break the bottom off each asparagus spear and rinse. Cut 3cm strips of prosciutto with scissors. Cut half of the camembert wheel into long, thin strips. Lay prosciutto flat horizontally, place one asparagus spear vertically on the meat. Lay a slice of camembert along the asparagus and roll the prosciutto around its contents. Place on a baking tray and bake in a 150C oven until the cheese has melted. Serve immediately.

Apricots & Blue Cheese

You will LOOOOOVE these!!

- *6 large fresh apricots*
- *Small block mild blue cheese*
- *12 walnuts, chopped*

Halve and stone small apricots and stuff with the mild blue cheese and walnuts.

Baked Brie with Peaches

- *250g brie cheese*
- *2 tbs. raspberry jam*
- *2 fresh peaches, peeled and diced*
- *1 tbs. brown sugar*

Preheat oven to 180C. Place brie in small shallow baking dish and evenly spread with jam. Top with peaches and sprinkle with brown sugar. Bake for 10 - 12 minutes or until the cheese softens.

Optional: Serve with crackers or fresh, crusty French bread slices.

Brie Bruschetta

- *1 crusty French stick, sliced 1 inch thick*
- *6 - 8 ripe tomatoes, chopped*
- *250g brie cheese*

Under grill, toast one side of the French bread slices. Remove and turn slices over. Brush un-toasted side with some of the juices that result when you chop the tomatoes. Lay slices of brie on the bread. Grill for a further 2 - 3 minutes until cheese has melted. Top with tomatoes and season with sea salt and pepper.

Cheese Pies

Makes 12. These little melt-in-the-mouth pies are best eaten warm.

- *2 sheets puff pastry*
- *200g mozzarella, grated*
- *200g feta cheese*
- *2 eggs, lightly beaten (reserve a little for basting)*

Cut 6 rounds from each sheet (use an upside down coffee cup). Place aside. In a bowl, mash the feta cheese with a fork, mix in mozzarella and then add the eggs. Put a tablespoon of the filling on one half of each round of pastry. Slightly dampen the pastry edges then fold the pastry over the filling to make a half-moon shape. Seal the by pressing down with the prongs of a fork and brush with reserved beaten egg. Place on a paper lined baking tray and bake them in a preheated oven at 200C for 15 - 20 minutes or until they are puffed and golden.

Chicken & Chorizo Skewers

Makes 6.

- *1 chicken breast, cubed*
- *1 chorizo sausage, sliced*
- *Extra virgin olive oil spray*
- *½ cup (125g) salsa*

Onto a skewer (or toothpick for a bite-sized serving) thread meats. Spray lightly before grilling. Serve warm with salsa as a dipping sauce.

Fried Camembert

This is sooooo easy and a real crowd pleaser!

* *250g camembert cheese*
* *1 egg*
* *4 tbs. fine breadcrumbs*
* *1 cup (250ml) peanut oil*

Cut chilled cheese into equal wedges. Lightly beat the egg and dip each cheese wedge, turning to coat. Roll in breadcrumbs. Cover and refrigerate. Deep-fry, turning regularly until golden brown in colour.

Optional: Add same quantity of sesame seeds to breadcrumbs for a little crunch. Serve with cranberry sauce.

Honey & Orange Prawns

A recipe from Susan Smith, Gold Coast.

* *24 fresh king prawns*
* *2 tsp. olive oil*
* *2 tbs. honey*
* *1 orange*

Peel and de-vein prawns. With the orange, finely grate 1 tbs. of zest and reserve 2 tbs. of orange juice. Combine oil, rind, juice and half the honey in a bowl, add prawns and marinate in the fridge for 1 hour. Cook in a hot, non-stick frypan until golden brown.

Optional: Serve with soy and ginger dipping sauce (see Sauces).

Hummus & Salad Tarts

A recipe from the gorgeous Kendra Horwood.

- *6 mini pastry cases (savoury)*
- *250g hummus*
- *100g mixed salad leaves (incl. herbs and edible flowers)*
- *1 tbs. lemon juice*

Combine lemon and salad, season with salt and pepper. Fill shells with hummus and pile the salad on top.

Mango Prawns

- *300g cooked king prawns*
- *2 stems fresh basil*
- *1 fresh mango*
- *100g prosciutto*

Peel prawns. De-vein and cut down the vein line, careful not to cut through. Flatten prawns slightly and lay a small basil leaf and sliver of mango over each prawn. Cut 2cm strips of prosciutto with scissors, wrap around each prawn and secure with a cocktail stick.

Optional: Rachael did these on soaked skewers and baked in 180C oven for 5 minutes, she sprinkled with chopped basil at the end and they were scrumptious!

Marinated & Baked Olives

- *500g green olives, pitted*
- *1 lemon*
- *2 sprigs rosemary*
- *2 cloves garlic, thinly sliced*

Preheat oven to 200C. Place olives in a baking dish and with a rolling pin, gently push down so skin splits. Onto the olives, grate the zest a lemon then add rosemary and garlic. Cook for 15 minutes and serve warm.

Optional: Add 1 tbs. olive oil to the mix.

Minted Lamb Balls

Serves 4. A recipe from Janelle McCosker.

- *500g minced lamb*
- *2 tsp. curry powder*
- *6 - 8 stems mint, chopped*

Mix all ingredients together and roll into bite-sized balls and fry in a non-stick frying pan until crunchy on the outside (this means they are cooked on the inside).

Optional: These are lovely served with sweet chilli as a dipping sauce.

Mozzarella Cubes

- *250g mozzarella cheese*
- *2 eggs*
- *22 Ritz crackers, crumbled*
- *¼ cup (60ml) extra virgin olive oil*

Cut mozzarella into 3cm cubes. Lightly beat the eggs, dip the cheese cubes into the egg and then into the cracker crumbs (for best result use a blender). Heat the oil in a frying pan and fry the cheese until golden brown.

Optional: Any soft, savoury cracker will do nicely.

Nin's Easy & Tasty Mushrooms

A recipe from Jan Neale, these are really easy and really nice!

- *12 medium sized mushrooms*
- *Sweet chilli sauce*
- *½ a wheel of Brie cheese*

Wash mushrooms and de-stalk. Place a dollop of sweet chilli sauce in the middle and top with a sliver of brie cheese. Place under warmed grill until brie melts.

Optional: Garnish with fresh herbs.

Pear & Roquefort Bites

- *2 fresh ripe pears, peeled and cubed*
- *125g Roquefort cheese, cubed*

Thread one cube of each onto a toothpick and serve immediately.

Quesadilla

Spanish and Speedy – sensational served with a corona and lime!!

- *4 flour tortilla*
- *4 tbs. tahini*
- *200g mozzarella, grated*
- *4 tsp. mixed herbs*

On tortillas, smear tahini and season with sea salt and pepper. Sprinkle on mozzarella and mixed herbs. Fold tortilla in half and gently press. Place in a 150C preheated oven and when cooked cut into wedges and serve.

Optional: Serve with salsa as a dipping sauce.

Sharchos (cousin of Nachos)

A t.e.r.r.i.f.i.c recipe from Sharon Webby.

- *250g cream cheese*
- *420g tin baked beans with sweet chilli sauce*
- *¾ cup (75g) cheddar cheese, grated*
- *1 pkt corn chips*

In a serving dish spread the cream cheese, top with the baked beans and sprinkle with cheese. Place under the grill until the cheese bubbles and is golden brown in colour. Serve warm with corn chips ... *Enjoy!*

Optional: If you can't find pre-mixed beans and chilli sauce, use a tin of ordinary baked beans and add 1 – 2 tbs. sweet chilli sauce.

Salmon Pittas

A timeless canapé from Kendra Horwood.

- *Mini pitta breads*
- *1 pkt smoked salmon*
- *250g crème fraîche*
- *Watercress*

Depending on size of your pittas, if quite thick cut in half or quarters. Top with smoked salmon, a dollop of crème fraîche and watercress to garnish.

Optional: Blinis work just as well as pitta breads.

Savoury Scrolls

A recipe from the beautiful Lisa Darr.

- *1 sheet puff pastry*
- *2 rashers bacon*
- *2 tbs. tomato paste*
- *⅓ cup (30g) parmesan cheese, grated*

Smooth tomato paste over the sheet of pastry. Scatter chopped bacon and cheese and roll into a log. Cut into pinwheels (2cm thick) and bake in a preheated 180C oven for 15 minutes or until pastry turns a golden brown.

Optional: Substitute tomato paste for pizza paste.

Spinach Cob

A beauty from Jocelyn Wilson.

- *1 cob loaf*
- *2 x 250g tubs sour cream*
- *1 pkt spring vegetable soup*
- *1 bunch fresh spinach or alternatively a 250g frozen spinach*

Boil enough spinach leaves to fill a cup, drain and allow to cool slightly. Mix sour cream, soup mix and spinach. Cook in microwave for 5 minutes. Combine and let favours develop for 15 minutes. Cut lid off cob loaf and scoop out the filling. Pour mixture into the cob and serve using the scooped filling to dip.

Strawberry Camembert Sticks

- *½ cup (125ml) balsamic vinegar*
- *1 punnet strawberries, washed and hulled*
- *125g camembert cheese*
- *Short bamboo skewers*

Simmer balsamic vinegar in a small pan until quite syrupy. Leave to cool. Thread strawberries and small wedges of camembert alternately onto skewers. Drizzle balsamic syrup over strawberries just before serving.

Strawberry Sweet & Sour

A recipe from Lorraine Leeson ... This will make an impact –
TRY IT!!!

* *1 punnet strawberries, washed*
* *¼ cup (55g) brown sugar*
* *½ cup (160g) sour cream*

Place brown sugar and sour cream in separate ramekins, dip a strawberry into sour cream and then into the sugar ... *It's like eating a caramelised strawberry.*

Tandoori Wings

D.e.l.i.c.i.o.u.s

* *1 kg chicken wings*
* *⅓ cup (75g) tandoori paste*
* *⅓ cup (85g) yoghurt*
* *1 medium brown onion, grated*

Preheat oven to 200C. Combine paste, yoghurt and onion in large bowl. Add chicken and coat generously. Cover and refrigerate for at least 3 hours. Place chicken on an oiled wire rack set inside larger shallow baking dish. Roast, uncovered in the oven for 30 minutes or until chicken is well browned and cooked through.

Tangy Cheese Balls

- 125g cream cheese
- ¼ cup (25g) blue cheese, finely crumbled
- 2 tbs. orange zest
- 100g mixed nuts, finely chopped

Combine cream cheese, blue cheese (add more if desired) and orange zest. Form into small balls and roll in nuts. Chill for an hour, or until firm, and serve.

Spanish Omelette

- 500g potatoes
- 4 eggs
- 2 tbs. extra virgin olive oil
- 1 onion, grated

Peel the potatoes, wash them thoroughly and cut into thin slices, season with sea salt. Heat oil in a frying pan and add the salted potatoes. Stir them until they are slightly browned. Add the onion and fry for 3 or 4 minutes. Beat the eggs and add to the mix. Brown one side and then turn to brown the other.

Spinach & Ricotta Scrolls

A recipe from the lovely Wendy Beattie.   Excellent entertainers!

- *250g frozen chopped spinach, thawed*
- *125g ricotta cheese*
- *100g mozzarella cheese, grated*
- *3 sheets puff pastry*

Combine spinach, which has been lightly squeezed to remove any excess water, and cheese and mix well. Season with sea salt and pepper. Halve each pastry sheet lengthways and then cut diagonally so you have 12 long triangular strips. Place a heaped tablespoon of mixture at the widest end and roll to enclose (forming triangular shapes). Place on a paper lined baking tray and bake in a preheated 180C oven for 20 - 25 minutes or until puffed and golden.

Optional: Baste with beaten egg for a really presentable finish.

Vegetable Wontons

A healthy, popular starter for all.

- *2 carrots, grated*
- *20g bean sprouts*
- *120g chopped, shredded vegetables of choice (sweet potato, zucchini, mushroom, cabbage are some great options)*
- *1 pkt Wonton Wrappers (around 10 papers)*

Combine all ingredients and place a tablespoon of mixture along the centre of each of the wanton papers. Roll up into small spring roll sized rolls, tucking in the sides as you roll. Steam for 6 - 8 minutes in a vegetable steamer. Serve warm.

Optional: Serve with sweet chilli sauce.

Morning & Afternoon Teas

Everyone smiles in the same language

Anonymous

Almond Bread Slice

Makes 15 slices. Recipe from Cyndi O'Meara.

- *4 eggwhites*
- *½ cup (110g) organic raw sugar*
- *1 cup (125g) organic plain flour*
- *200g almonds*

Preheat oven to 180C. Beat egg whites until stiff, add sugar and beat for 1 minute. Stir in flour and almonds. Place mixture in paper lined loaf tin and bake for 40 minutes. When cool, slice thinly. Place slices on a baking tray, return to oven until browned (10 - 15 minutes).

Black Forest Cake

Serves 8. Recipe from Miranda Kunde.

- *1 double chocolate sponge cake*
- *600ml double cream with brandy*
- *1½ x 260g cans of pitted cherries in natural juice*

Break the cake into small pieces and spread a layer into the base of a jelly ring (or other round flexible container). Sprinkle some cherries and juice over the top. Spoon a layer of cream over the cake. Repeat the process until all ingredients are used. Place in the fridge for 4 hours to set or until firm.

Caramel Ginger Tarts

**Makes 12. A recipe from Jennette McCosker ...
Easy and Economical!**

- *12 ginger nut bickies*
- *400g can condensed milk*
- *½ cup (125ml) cream, whipped*
- *1 banana*

Place unopened tin of condensed milk into a large saucepan generously covering tin with water, boil for 2½ hours to turn the milk into caramel, (check every 30 minutes to ensure tin is covered in water, top up when necessary so the tin doesn't burst). Meanwhile place cookies on the individual circles of a patty cake tin and bake in 150C oven for 10 minutes. Remove and gently mould the softened bickies into patty cake shells. When cool, add enough cooled caramel to fill the bickie. Top with whipped cream and a slice or two of banana as garnish.

Tip: Nestle do have a tin of Caramel Top 'n' Fill which is a premade tin of caramel ... Sooo easy and sooo yummy, ask you local supermarket if they can get it in!

Chocolate Lychees

A recipe from Meg Wilson. These are elegant, easy & amazing with coffee.

- *110g milk chocolate*
- *¼ cup (62ml) cream*
- *16 fresh lychees, peeled and de-seeded*

Melt chocolate add ¼ cup of cream and mix well. Dip lychees, coating well and set in fridge.

Optional: If not in season, tinned lychees work just as well.

Chocolate Parcels

Makes 25. Recipe from Cyndi O'Meara … Y.U.M!

- *250g dark chocolate*
- *200g blanched almonds, halved and lightly toasted*
- *50g glazed ginger, chopped*

Melt chocolate in a double boiler, stirring constantly. Remove from heat as soon as completely melted. Add almonds and ginger to the melted chocolate and mix well. Spoon small amounts 2cm apart on a paper lined baking tray. Refrigerate until hardened then serve. Store parcels in an airtight container and refrigerate.

Coconut Mini Muffins

Makes 12

- *½ cup (60g) coconut*
- *½ cup (125ml) milk*
- *½ cup (100g) caster sugar*
- *½ cup (85g) self raising flour*

Preheat oven to 180C. Place all ingredients in a bowl and mix. Line a mini muffin tray with patty papers and distribute mixture evenly. Bake for 15 minutes.

Optional: Top with our incredibly easy white chocolate ganache.

Cream Cheese Icing

- *1 tbs. butter*
- *2 - 3 tbs. cream cheese*
- *1 tsp. lemon zest (optional)*
- *1 cup (120g) icing sugar*

Soften butter. Add cream cheese and beat well. Add lemon zest and sifted icing sugar (you may need a little more). Continue to beat until icing is nice and smooth.

Crostoli

A recipe from Jan Neale 'Nin'. These are delicious served with coffee.

- *1 sheet shortcrust pastry*
- *1 cup (250ml) vegetable oil*
- *2 - 3 tbs. cinnamon sugar*

Cut pastry into 1½ cm strips twist and place on a paper lined baking tray. Freeze for 10 - 15 minutes. Heat oil on high, it is ready when a piece of pastry sizzles in it. Deep fry the twists in batches, turning once until golden. Remove and place on draining paper. Whilst hot, coat well with cinnamon sugar.

Optional: Dust with icing sugar for presentation.

Coconut Macaroons

Makes 25 - 30. Recipe from Lisa Hayes.

- *2 eggs, separated*
- *¾ cup (165g) organic sugar*
- *360g organic desiccated coconut*

Preheat oven to 180C. Add a pinch of salt to eggwhites, and beat until soft peaks form. Beat in egg yolks one at a time, gradually add sugar, beating well after each addition. Stir in coconut and mix well. Spoon tablespoons of mixture onto alfoil lined trays. Bake for 8 minutes, or until golden brown.

Flourless Chocolate Cake

- *4 eggs*
- *200g butter*
- *250g dark chocolate*
- *1 cup (200g) caster sugar*

Preheat oven 180C. Separate eggs, add ½ the sugar to the yolks and beat well with a mixer. Beat egg whites until fluffy then add remaining sugar, gradually beating until stiff peaks form. Melt butter and chocolate over hot water stirring regularly. Pour into egg yolk mixture and fold. Once combined fold in egg whites. Line a cake tin with greaseproof paper and pour in mixture. Bake in a 22cm cake tin for 40 minutes in the lower third of your oven.
Note: This cake will collapse and the top will flake, as it has no flour to sustain the rise but it is gorgeous and a favourite for all.

Optional: Can be served warm or cold and is delicious with fresh whipped cream.

Fruit Cake

Serves 4. Recipe from Jen Whittington ... *Delicious!*

* *1kg mixed fruit*
* *2 cups (500ml) fruit juice or cold organic tea of choice*
* *2 cups (350g) organic self raising flour*

Preheat oven to 125C. Soak fruits in juice or tea overnight. Stir flour into soaked fruit and mix well. Spoon mixture into a 22cm lined cake tin. Bake for 2 – 2½ hours in the bottom of your oven or until cooked through. Remove and leave to cool. Place in an air tight container or wrap in alfoil.

Tip: This cake can be frozen.

Optional: Add a shot of your favourite tipple, sherry, brandy, rum, grand marnier.

Fruit Mince Palmiers

* *2 tbs. raw sugar*
* *1 sheet puff pastry*
* *2 - 3 tbs. fruit mince*

Preheat oven to 200C. Line a baking tray with baking paper and sprinkle sugar onto it. Lay pastry on the paper and spread the entire surface with mince. Roll up one side tightly until you reach the middle then repeat with the other side. Freeze for 30 minutes before removing and slicing into 1cm thick slices. Bake for 15 – 20 minutes or until golden brown.

Gingered Prunes

Serves 4. By Jocelyn Wilson … These are real treats!

- *250g prunes pips removed*
- *225ml cream*
- *50g crystallized ginger*
- *1 tbs. icing sugar*

Finely dice the crystallized ginger. Combine cream, ginger and icing sugar. Fill the centre of each prune. Serve chilled.

Jam Tarts

- *1 sheet short crust pastry*
- *1 tbs. butter*
- *Jam of choice*

Lay pastry flat and cut as many circles as possible, press each circle into a lightly buttered patty cake tin, pressing a fork down around the edges for decoration. Cook at 180C for around 10 minutes. Spoon the desired amount of jam into each tart, return to the oven for another five minutes.

Optional: Top with a dollop of freshly whipped cream.

Kisses

- ½ cup (115g) butter (reserve a tsp.)
- 1 cup (175g) self raising flour
- 1 tbs. icing sugar
- 1 tbs. arrowroot

Preheat oven to 150C. Cream butter and sugar and add arrowroot and flour. Grease a baking tray with reserved butter, scoop a teaspoon full onto a paper lined tray and press with a fork. Cook till pale brown.

Optional: Join two together with some jam or icing when cool.

Mandarin & Almond Cake

**And who says you learn nothing at Work Conferences …
Thanks, Fiona Burt!**

- 3 mandarins
- 1 cup (220g) sugar
- 6 eggs
- 2 cups (340g) almond meal

Cover mandarins (skin and all) with water, bring to boil then simmer for 1 hour. Cool completely, remove seeds and puree. Beat eggs and sugar together, add puree and almond meal. Stir well, pour into a greased 22cm cake tin and bake at 160C for 70 minutes.

Optional: Kelly Mauger, a 'Dynamite Chef' at Bella Boo Café in Mundubbera, Australia advised that you can substitute mandarins with apples, bananas or oranges. She made it with oranges, topped with cream cheese icing and sprinkled with poppy seeds…BEEEEEUUUUUUUTIFUL!!

Meringues

- *2 eggwhites*
- *½ cup (100g) caster sugar*
- *¼ tsp. vanilla*
- *1 tbs. butter*

Preheat oven 150C. Whip eggwhites till stiff then gradually add sugar and vanilla, continuing to beat. Place in dessert spoonfuls onto a well greased (use butter) baking tray. Bake in oven until dry and firm.

Tip: If eggwhites are allowed to stand overnight they will whip up nicely. A pinch of salt in eggwhites makes them stiffen quickly. To prevent a meringue top shrinking and becoming moist after cooking, sift a dusting of icing sugar over the meringue before placing in the oven.

Oreo Cake

A recipe perfected by Georgia Darr, 10 years old!

- *340g pkt white cake mix*
- *⅓ cup oil*
- *2 eggs*
- *150g pkt Oreo biscuits, crushed*

Preheat oven 180C. Mix first 3 ingredients with 1 cup water and mix with a beater until combined. Add biscuits and fold in with a spoon. Pour mixture into a paper lined 22cm cake tin. Bake for 40 minutes. Remove and allow to completely cool before icing.

Optional: This is delicious iced with chocolate ganache.

Peanut Butter Cookies

Makes around 20 ... Gluten-free and *glorious*!

- *1 cup (260g) crunchy peanut butter*
- *1 cup (220g) brown sugar*
- *1 tsp. cinnamon*
- *1 egg*

Preheat oven to 180C. Mix all ingredients into a bowl. Spoon small tablespoon sized balls onto 2 lined baking trays. Slightly flatten with a fork, crisscross style. Bake for 8 minutes, or until a thin crust forms on the cookie.

Optional: Robyn Mayeke suggested that these work just as well without cinnamon, store well and "the kids love them!"

Pecan Pie

Serves 6. This is really easy and really nice!

- *3 eggwhites*
- *1 cup (200g) caster sugar*
- *1 cup (100g) pecan nuts, chopped*
- *22 Ritz crackers, crushed*

Beat eggwhites until stiff, gently adding caster sugar throughout. Fold in chopped pecan nuts and crushed crackers. Pour mixture into a pie dish and bake in a preheated 180C oven for 25 minutes.

Optional: Add a dash of vanilla essence. Slice as you would a cheesecake and top with a dollop of whipped cream and piece of seasonal fruit.

Pineapple Cake

A recipe by Brett McCosker.   2 words – *TRY IT!!!*

- *2 cups (350g) self raising flour*
- *1 cup (200g) caster sugar*
- *432g tin crushed pineapple*

Sift flour into a mixing bowl and combine with sugar. Add pineapple (entire contents of the tin) and mix well. Pour into a greased 22cm cake tin and bake at 180C for 40 minutes.

Pineapple Cake Icing

- *400g condensed milk*
- *⅓ cup (70g) butter, melted*
- *1 cup (120g) shredded coconut*
- *½ tsp. vanilla*

Combine condensed milk and melted butter and bring to boil. Stirring constantly, boil for 4 minutes. Add coconut and mix. While mixture is hot, spread over cooled cake.

Optional: The above amounts cover the entire cake, lid and sides. If however you just want to cover the lid use half of the ingredients.

Rocky Road

A recipe by Jennette McCosker ... Kim's favourite!!!

- *250g milk chocolate*
- *100g macadamia nuts, roughly chopped*
- *1 cup marshmallows, cut in half*
- *1 cup Turkish delight, roughly chopped*

Break chocolate into pieces and melt in microwave on medium high stirring every 20 seconds. Allow to cool slightly before adding remaining ingredients. Mix until well combined. Line a small rectangular dish with baking paper, pour the mixture into it, neaten edges and refrigerate until set. Cut into desired serving pieces.

Optional: Use nut of choice, almond, hazelnut, Brazil nut etc.

Rum Balls I

Makes 15. An absolute treasure from Anthony 'Spud' Moore.

- *500g moist Christmas cake or heavy fruit cake*
- *½ cup (125ml) dark rum*
- *250g dark chocolate*
- *1 cup (120g) desiccated coconut*

Place Christmas cake and rum in a food processor and blend until combined. Allow to stand for 30 minutes in fridge. Melt chocolate. Roll cake mix into balls, roll in chocolate then in coconut. Place on a tray and chill before serving.

Rum Balls II

Thanks for the idea Russell Halfpenny.

- *8 Weetabix, crushed*
- *3 tbs. dark rum*
- *400g can condensed milk*
- *1 cup (120g) desiccated coconut*

Mix all ingredients, except ¼ cup of coconut. Add rum and condensed milk. Mix thoroughly (add extra Weetabix if required). Shape into balls and roll in extra coconut. Store in fridge.

Optional: Add 1 cup (220g) of mixed fruit to the dry ingredients and reduce Weetabix to 6.

Scones

Makes 12. A recipe from the kitchen wonder herself, Daphne Beutel ... It doesn't get any easier!

- *700g self raising flour*
- *300ml cream*
- *375ml can lemonade*

Sift self raising flour into a bowl, make a well and pour in cream and lemonade. Mix to make a firm dough, roll out and cut with a scone cutter. Arrange closely together on a paper lined baking tray and bake in a preheated 220C oven until golden brown (approx. 12 minutes).

Shortbread

A recipe by the lovely Jennette McCosker.

- ½ cup (115g) butter
- ½ cup (85g) plain flour
- 3 tbs. cornflour
- 3 tbs. icing sugar

Preheat oven to 180C. Mix altogether in a blender. Press into baking tray lined with baking paper. Bake for 30 minutes.

Strawberry Pie

- 1 cup (320g) sour cream
- 1 cup (250ml) milk
- 2 pkt angel delight strawberry
- 1 readymade sweet pie base

Beat sour cream and milk until smooth, add 1½ pkt. pudding mix and continue beating slowly until mixture thickens (add remaining if required). Pour into pre-bought pie base mix and chill for an hour.

Optional: Serve PILED high with lots of delicious, fresh raspberries.

Ultimate Caramel Macadamia Tart

Rach's Dad, Billy Moore's absolute favourite!

- *1 sheet short crust pastry*
- *400g can condensed milk*
- *100g dark cooking chocolate*
- *100g macadamia nuts, chopped and roasted*

Place unopened tin of condensed milk into a large saucepan covered with water, boil for 2½ hours to turn the milk into caramel, (check every 30 minutes to ensure tin is covered in water, top up when necessary so the tin doesn't burst). Preheat oven to 180C. Cut pastry into 4 squares and mould into greased muffin tin (or alternatively cut into 16ths and mould into mini-muffin shells). Bake for 8 - 10 minutes or until lightly golden brown. Melt chocolate in a microwave, stirring every 15 seconds and brush pastry shells internally. Allow chocolate to cool before spooning *cooled* caramel into the shells and topping with the roasted macadamia nuts.

Tip: Nestle do have a tin of Caramel Top 'n' Fill which is a premade tin of caramel ... Sooo easy and sooo yummy, ask you local supermarket if they can get it in!

White Chocolate Ganache

- *150g white chocolate*
- *½ cup (160ml) sour cream*

In a microwave, melt chocolate stirring every 20 seconds until nice and smooth. Allow to cool slightly and mix in sour cream.

Optional: Substitute white chocolate for milk or dark chocolate.

Light Meals & Lunches

Worries go down better with soup

Jewish Proverb

Soups

Asparagus Soup

Serves 4 - 6

- *400g can asparagus tips*
- *400g tin cream of chicken soup*

Mix all ingredients plus 1 cup (250ml) of water, heat until boiling. Serve with toasted bread fingers and a few asparagus tips as garnish.

Carrot & Coriander Soup

Serves 4

- *2 ltr. vegetable stock*
- *1 large onion, chopped*
- *6 stems fresh coriander, roots included*
- *8 carrots, roughly chopped*

Heat vegetable stock so that it is warm. Add roughly chopped coriander leaves and roots, onion and carrots. Bring to the boil, reduce heat and simmer until the carrots are tender. Season with sea salt and pepper before blending.

Optional: Before serving swirl through some sour cream if desired.

Chestnut & Vegetable Soup

Serves 4 - 6

- *250g peeled chestnuts*
- *1½ ltr. chicken stock*
- *500g ptk butternut squash & sweet potato*
- *1 - 2 tbs. butter*

Saute squash and sweet potato and chestnuts in butter until lightly browned, add stock and simmer for one hour. Using a hand held blender, blend until smooth, season to taste.

Chilled Melon Soup

Serves 6. A real delight on a hot summer night!

- *1 medium rock melon*
- *½ honeydew melon*
- *½ cup (125ml) sparkling grape or pear juice, chilled*
- *6 strawberries washed, hulled and quartered*

Blend rock melon in food processor until smooth. Add sparkling grape juice and blend quickly to combine. Serve immediately in bowls with diced honeydew, strawberries and crushed ice.

Kim's French Onion Soup

Serves 2

- *2 large onions, peeled and coarsely chopped*
- *2 zucchinis (courgettes), coarsely chopped*
- *1 pkt French onion soup*
- *½ cup (125ml) cream*

Place onions, zucchini and soup mix in a saucepan with 4 cups of water, season with pepper and boil, reduce heat by half and leave for 30 minutes stirring occasionally. Blend till smooth, add cream, stir and serve.

Optional: Grill some tasty cheese on a thick slice of French stick and place in middle of the soup before serving.

Pea & Ham Soup

Serves 4 - 6

- *750ml chicken stock*
- *500g frozen peas*
- *5 fresh sage leaves*
- *1 ham steak*

Bring stock to boil. Add peas and sage leaves and cook for 5 minutes. Place in a blender or food processor and process until smooth. Return to saucepan. Remove rind from ham. Chop flesh very finely. Mix into soup and bring to the boil.

Optional: Serve hot with crusty bread.

Pumpkin Soup

Serves 4 - 6. A recipe from Lisa Darr. Fabulously fast and flavoursome!

- *½ pumpkin, skinned & thinly sliced*
- *5 chicken stock cubes*
- *1 large brown onion*

Place all ingredients into a saucepan. Add enough water to cover pumpkin then boil until ingredients are soft. Blend until smooth.

Optional: Serve with a generous dollop of sour cream.

Salmon & Asparagus Soup

Serves 6. A recipe from Alexis Wallis. An amazing entertainer for very little effort!

- *400g tin cream of asparagus soup*
- *220g can red salmon*
- *300ml cream*

Drain salmon, removing skin and bones before pureeing in a blender. In a saucepan, mix salmon with soup and 1 cup water. Add cream to the mixture and heat without boiling, season with pepper if desired.

Sweet Potato & Pear Soup

Serves 4 - 6

- *1 large sweet potato (white flesh, purple jacket)*
- *2 medium pears*
- *2 chicken stock cubes*

Peel and chop sweet potato and pears, place in a saucepan, cover with water and stock cubes. Cook until softened, cool slightly before blending.

Thai Pumpkin Soup

Serves 4. A recipe from Anthony 'Spud' Moore. *THAI-RRIFIC!!*

- *1kg butternut pumpkin (butternut squash), peeled and diced*
- *2 tbs. red curry paste*
- *300ml coconut cream*
- *3 stems fresh coriander, chopped*

Sauté pumpkin and red curry paste until it starts to catch on the saucepan. Add coconut cream to deglaze the pan, top with enough water to level with the pumpkin and bring to boil. Reduce heat simmering until the pumpkin becomes soft and mushy. Puree, season with sea salt and pepper and fold in chopped coriander.

Vitamin C Soup

Serves 4. Another from Kim's clever Mummy, Jennette McCosker.

- *400g tin cream of tomato soup*
- *1 orange*
- *3 tbs. cream*

Juice the orange and then finely grate the rind. Place soup in a saucepan. Combine orange juice and sufficient water to make one can of liquid, and add to soup. Stir in orange zest and bring soup to boil. Remove from heat, stir in cream and serve immediately.

Zucchini Soup

Serves 2. A recipe from Jen Whittington.

- *1 zucchini (courgette)*
- *1 onion, peeled and coarsely chopped*
- *1 pkt chicken soup*

Boil the vegetables together for 30 minutes. Drain half the water, add the dry soup and blend till smooth. Season with pepper and serve.

All Others

After 30, a body has a mind of its own!

Bette Midler

Antipasto Tart

Makes 12 and are scrumptious!

- *2 sheets puff pastry*
- *250g antipasto mix*
- *3 eggs*
- *320g sour cream*

Use a large cup to cut 12 rounds from your puff pastry sheets. Line a non-stick muffin tray with the rounds. Divide the antipasto mix between each. Lightly whisk eggs, add sour cream, season with sea salt and pepper. Pour over tarts and bake in a 180C oven for 20 minutes.

Optional: Add a splash of tomato and Worcestershire sauces to the egg mix. Top with a sprinkle of parmesan cheese.

Asparagus Soufflé

Serves 4

- *2 tbs. butter*
- *3 tbs. flour*
- *400g tin cream of asparagus soup*
- *4 eggs, separated*

Preheat oven to 180C. Melt butter in a saucepan and remove from heat. Stir in flour until a pasty texture. Stir in undiluted soup. Beat in egg yolks, one at a time. Beat eggwhites until stiff and then fold into mixture, quickly and lightly. Pour into a greased soufflé dish and bake for 30 – 35 minutes.

Optional: Can substitute celery soup for asparagus.

Bacon Pizza

Serves 1. A recipe from the lovely Veronica Griffin.

- *1 pitta bread or Lebanese bread*
- *3 tbs. pizza sauce*
- *3 rashers bacon*
- *¼ cup (25g) mozzarella cheese, grated*

Finely dice bacon and fry for 2 minutes. Spread pizza sauce on pitta bread, sprinkle with bacon and top with mozzarella cheese. Place in a moderate oven under the grill until the cheese browns.
To maintain crisp bread, place directly onto oven racks.

Beef Koftas

Makes 4 - 6

- *½ cup (130g) crunchy peanut butter*
- *2 tsp. curry powder*
- *1 egg*
- *500g lean beef mince*

Warm peanut butter in a microwave on high for 20 seconds to soften. Mix in curry powder and egg. Add to mince and combine. Roll mixture into fat sausage shapes using ½ cup of mixture for each kofta. Grill or BBQ until cooked.

Optional: Serve as a burger or on pitta bread with satay sauce and salad or separately as a patty with vegetables ... mmmmm!

Beef Samosas

Makes 18

- *30g curry paste*
- *120ml apple juice*
- *500g mince*
- *3 sheets frozen puff pastry, thawed*

Preheat oven to 180C. Add 2 tbs. water to a non-stick frying pan then brown mince. Mix curry paste with apple juice until smooth, then add to mince. Simmer mixture for 6 – 8 minutes, stirring occasionally and add more apple juice if needed. Cut 6 large circles from your pastry sheets. Dollop a generrours tbs. of mince on one half of the circle. Fold the other half over the mixture creating a semi-circular roll. Seal edges firmly with a fork and place onto a paper lined baking tray. Bake for 20 minutes or until golden brown.

Optional: Serve with sweet-chilli sauce as dipping sauce. Add any number of grated vegetables to it if desired, chunks of potatoes or beans are nice for a change to.

Cheese & Garlic Pizza

Serves 2. Another recipe from Anthony 'Spud' Moore.

- *3 tortilla rounds*
- *16 cloves garlic*
- *100g parmesan cheese, grated*
- *100g mozzarella cheese, grated*

Preheat oven 230C. Peel garlic, wrap in alfoil and roast in oven for 15 minutes. Remove and cool. Lay one tortilla flat and spread ⅓ garlic, ⅓ parmesan and ⅓ mozzarella. Lay second tortilla on top and repeat process, lay third tortilla on top and repeat process. Cook for 15 minutes or until cheese bubbles and turns golden brown. Slice into wedges to serve.

Coronation Chicken Pittas

Makes 2

- *2 pitta breads, split and toasted*
- *90g jar Coronation chicken*
- *100g mixed salad leaves*
- *2 stems fresh coriander*

Fill pittas with as much coronation chicken as desired. Stuff with mixed lettuce leaves and a generous amount of fresh coriander.

Gourmet Pizza

Serves 1. A recipe from Karyn Turnbull-Markus.

* *3 tbs. peach chutney*
* *Lebanese bread*
* *3 slices prosciutto*
* *3 rounds baby bocconcini*

Spread the peach chutney over the Lebanese bread, tear prosciutto & bocconcini into strips and place on top of pizza, then place directly onto oven racks for a crispy finish. Bake in a preheated 180C oven for 10 - 15 minutes.

Optional: Mango or fruit chutney works just as nicely.

Healthy Hamburger

Serves 4

* *4 organic scotch beef burgers*
* *4 rye bread rolls*
* *100g cheddar cheese, grated*
* *Shredded lettuce*

Grill or BBQ meat patties. Cut rolls in half. Sprinkle cheese onto both halves of roll. Add meat patties to lower side and top with lettuce.

Optional: Serve with a dollop of avocado salsa (see Dips).

Healthy Hotdogs

Serves 4

- *4 wraps*
- *4 organic sausages*
- *100g cheddar cheese, grated*
- *1 carrot, shredded or diced tomato or fried sliced onion*

Grill or BBQ sausages. Lay wraps out and sprinkle equal portions of cheese onto each. Add chosen vegetable and rollup.

Optional: Serve with tomato or BBQ sauce.

Jacket Potato with Chilli Con Carne

Serves 4

- *4 large potatoes*
- *400g can medium chilli con carne, heated*
- *¼ cup (80g) sour cream*
- *1 tbs. chopped fresh chives*

Pierce potato with knife several times then wrap it in foil, bake in preheated 180C oven for 40 minutes, or until soft. Remove from oven, stand for 5 minutes, remove alfoil and cut a crisscross into the potato, half way through. Top with chilli con carne, a dollop of sour cream and freshly cut chives.

Jacket Potato with Tomato Salsa

Serves 1

- *1 large potato (200g)*
- *2 tbs. tomato salsa*
- *¼ cup (55g) cottage cheese*
- *1 tbs. chopped fresh chives*

Pierce potato with knife several times. Wrap potato in alfoil, bake in preheated 180C oven for 40 minutes, or until soft. Remove from oven, stand for 5 minutes, remove alfoil and cut a crisscross into the potato, half way through. Add cottage cheese, top with salsa and sprinkle with chives.

Oysters Kilpatrick

- *6 oysters*
- *1 bacon rasher*
- *2 tbs. BBQ sauce*
- *2 tbs. tomato sauce*

Preheat grill 230C. Place washed oysters on baking tray. Dice bacon finely and mix with the combined sauces. Spoon the mixture onto oysters and grill until oysters begin to bubble and bacon is crisp but not burnt.

Oysters Mexicano

- *6 oysters*
- *½ lime, juiced*
- *12 corn chips*
- *¼ cup (55g) guacamole*

Place washed oysters on serving plate and pour lime evenly over them. Spoon on guacamole and stud with a corn chip for serving.

Oysters Champagne

- *6 oysters*
- *¼ tsp. minced ginger*
- *4 tbs. champagne*
- *¼ tsp. chopped mint*

Place washed oysters on serving plate. Combine remaining ingredients and spoon over oysters. Serve immediately.

Thanks 'Spud' for the above ever popular oyster recipes.

Salt & Pepper Calamari

Serves 6. Y.u.m.m.y!

- *1 tsp. Sichuan peppercorns and 1 tsp. sea salt*
- *400g fresh calamari*
- *1 cup (120g) cornflour*
- *1 cup (250ml) vegetable oil*

In a dry pan, roast the peppercorns until they become fragrant and begin to crackle, transfer to a mortar along with sea salt and grind. Add cornflour and roll the calamari in the mixture, shake off any excess. Deep fry in a hot wok for 1 minute or until cooked. Drain and serve hot.

Optional: Sichuan peppercorns can be substituted with mixed peppercorns.

Sausage Rolls

Serves 2 - 4.   Y.u.m.m.y y.u.m.m.y !!

- *2 sheets puff pastry*
- *250g lean mince*
- *1 onion*
- *1 tbs. oxo*

Preheat oven 180C. Place mince and chopped onion with slightly less than ¼ cup water into a saucepan. Season generously with sea salt and pepper. Cook until mince is brown. Add oxo and stir until combined, allow to cool. Place each sheet of pastry onto paper lined baking trays. Spoon mince down the centre of each sheet, brush sides of pastry with water and roll up. Cut into desired thickness. Bake for 20 minutes or until pastry is nice and golden.

Optional: Add ½ tsp. mixed herbs to the mince for flavor. Add a chopped tomato or whatever vegetable you like for a change.

Sweet Chilli Chicken Wrap

Serves 1

- *1 wrap*
- *1 chicken thigh*
- *1 tbs. sweet chilli sauce*
- *2 tsp. soy sauce*

Chop chicken thigh into chunks, throw into a heated, non-stick pan with sweet chilli sauce and soy sauce. Toss this mix until the chicken is cooked, which takes between 5 - 10 minutes. Heat the tortilla under a grill for 3 minutes. Once warm, place the cooked chicken on the tortilla and add whatever else you would like in the wrap.

Optional: Add fresh coriander to sweet chilli and soy sauce mix.

Sweet Guacamole Wrap

Serves 4 – 6. You will be pleasantly surprised!

- *1 pkt wholemeal wraps*
- *1½ cups (150g) grated cheddar cheese*
- *2 ripe avocados*
- *1 sweet potato*

Peel and thinly slice sweet potato and gently steam until soft throughout then remove from heat. Spoon out avocado flesh into a small bowl, discarding shell and skin, mash flesh with a fork. Lay each wrap flat and spread 1 tbs. of avocado onto the surface, leaving an inch bare around the perimeter. Place 3 slices of the still warm sweet potato evenly onto the avocado surface. Sprinkle 2 tbs. of grated cheese onto the sweet potato. Roll wraps into logs and serve.

Vegetarian Pizza

Serves 1

- *1 wholemeal pitta bread*
- *2 tbs. pizza sauce*
- *Mixed, sliced vegetables (pumpkin, onion, red pepper, eggplant, corn whatever you have in the fridge)*
- *50g mozzarella cheese, grated*

Select your veges, slice and grill or bake in the oven until almost soft. Spread pizza sauce on pitta bread, top with vegetables and sprinkle with mozzarella cheese. Place under grill at 180C until cheese browns. For crispy bread, place pitta bread directly onto oven rack.

Optional: Mix 1 tsp. basil pesto with the pizza sauce … yummy!

Sides

Take care of your body. It's the only place you have to live.

Jim Rohn

Salads

Baby Spinach & Strawberry Salad

Serves 4

- *200g fresh baby spinach leaves*
- *2 punnets strawberries washed, hulled and sliced*
- *50g sunflower seeds*

Place washed baby spinach in a bowl and add strawberries. Top the salad with cooled, dry-roasted sunflower seeds (spread on a baking tray and toast in a preheated oven 180C, stirring occasionally, for about 3 minutes) drizzle with suggested salad dressing.

NB: This salad is beautiful drizzled with Spinach & Strawberry Salad Dressing (see Salad Dressings).

Basil & Lentil Salad

Recipe from Shea Moor ... Tis Grand!

- *2 fresh bunches of basil*
- *400g tin of brown lentils, drained*
- *1 punnet of cherry tomatoes, halved*
- *½ Spanish onion, thinly sliced*

Tear basil leaves from stem and place in a salad bowl. Add remaining ingredients and toss to combine.

Optional: Serve drizzled with the Classic Salad Dressing (see Salad Dressing).

Curried Eggs

- *6 hardboiled eggs*
- *2 tbs. whole egg mayonnaise*
- *½ tsp. curry powder*
- *½ tsp. finely chopped parsley*

Peel eggs and cut in half lengthwise. Remove yolks and mash. Add mayonnaise, curry powder, parsley and season with sea salt and pepper. Place yolk mixture back into the egg halves.

Mango, Avocado & Bacon Salad

Serves 4. This trio is a KNOCKOUT!!

- *2 large mangoes*
- *2 avocados*
- *8 rashers of cooked, crispy bacon*

Cube mangoes and avocados, cut bacon in largish chunks and mix together in a small bowl.

Orange & Almond Salad

Serves 4

- *½ iceberg lettuce, shredded*
- *2 oranges, peeled and sliced*
- *4 bacon rashers*
- *100g blanched almonds, chopped and toasted*

Fry bacon until crispy, cool and cut roughly. Combine all ingredients in a salad bowl. Refrigerate until ready to serve.

Optional: Dress with a balsamic vinaigrette.

Prawn & Avocado Salad

Serves 2

- *100g mixed lettuce*
- *1 large avocado, peeled and sliced*
- *200g uncooked prawns, peeled and de-veined*
- *2 tbs. thousand island dressing*

Arrange lettuce, avocado and prawns on two plates, drizzle with dressing.

Optional: Add 1 mango cubed and ¼ cup macadamia nuts, lightly toasted and chopped.

Red Salad

A recipe from Perditta O'Connor; a fabulous addition to any BBQ!

- *1kg watermelon, sliced*
- *½ Spanish onion, thinly sliced*
- *2 tbs. balsamic vinegar*

Layer watermelon and onion in a serving dish and drizzle with balsamic vinegar.

Salmon & Caper Salad

Serves 4

- *100g tin drained salmon*
- *100g feta crumbled*
- *200g rocket (or other salad greens)*
- *1 tbs. drained capers, chopped*

Simply mix and enjoy!

Thai Chilli Mango Squid Salad

Serves 4. A recipe from Spud Moore. "This is the tastiest salad ever!"… Rach.

- *200g rocket lettuce*
- *500g squid cleaned*
- *1 large ripe mango*
- *250ml Thai chilli sauce*

Cut squid tubes into triangles. Marinate with Thai chilli sauce for 1 hour. De-seed and skin the mango, slice and place in a serving bowl. Pan fry squid quickly and add to mango, top with rocket and serve.

Waldorf Salad

Serves 4

* *3 seasonal apples, diced*
* *150g raisins*
* *100g pecan nuts, chopped*
* *½ cup (130g) whole egg mayonnaise*

In a bowl, combine ingredients and refrigerate until ready to serve.

Watermelon Salad

Serves 4. A recipe from Karyn Turnbull-Markus.
This is sensational!

* *4 tbs. balsamic vinegar*
* *½ watermelon*
* *1 punnet cherry tomatoes, cut in half*
* *½ cup (60g) crushed pistachios*

Cut watermelon into edible chunks, BBQ till grill marks appear on the melon. Move to a serving bowl and sprinkle with cherry tomatoes, nuts and balsamic vinegar.

Potato

Did you know: Francisco Pizarro found the potato in Ecuador and brought them to Spain in the early sixteenth century!

Bombay Potatoes

Makes 4

- *1 tbs. Garam masala curry powder*
- *400g can chopped tomatoes*
- *1 vegetable stock cube made up with 150ml boiling water*
- *8 - 10 potatoes, cut into 2cm cubes*

Fry onions in a little water for 4 - 5 minutes until soft. Add garam masala and fry for a further 1 - 2 minutes. Add the tomatoes and stock and bring to the boil. Stir in potatoes, cover and simmer for 25 - 30 minutes or until tender, stirring occasionally.

Garlic Potato

Serves 4

- *4 large potatoes, peeled and cut into 1cm slices*
- *320g sour cream*
- *200g mozzarella cheese, grated (reserve a little)*
- *2 cloves garlic, crushed*

Preheat oven 180C. Lightly steam potatoes for 15 minutes, or until just soft, set aside. Combine cheese, garlic and sour cream in a bowl. Line a baking dish with the steamed potato, keeping ¼ aside. Alternate a layer of potatoes with garlic, sour cream and cheese combination, ending with the liquid combo. Top with reserved cheese and bake for 30 minutes.

Mashed Potato with Pine Nuts

Serves 4

- *4 medium potatoes*
- *2 tbs. butter*
- *¼ cup (60ml) milk*
- *50g pine nuts, toasted*

Peel potatoes and cut each into 4 even pieces. Microwave potatoes until tender, drain and mash well. Add butter and milk, beating until butter is melted. Add pine nuts and mix well.

Optional: For additional flavour, add 1 tsp. dried rosemary.

Oven Roasted Wedges

Serves 4 - 6. Recipe from Cyndi O'Meara.

- *6 medium potatoes, unpeeled and cut into wedges*
- *3 tbs. cold pressed macadamia nut oil*
- *1 tsp. dried oregano*
- *1 tsp. sea salt*

Preheat oven 200C. Place potatoes in a large baking dish, drizzle with oil and coat well. Bake for 20 - 30 minutes or until browned. Add salt and oregano, toss well and serve.

'Point it to a Window' Mashed Potatoes

Serves 4. A third generation recipe from the Wilson family.

- *4 potatoes*
- *⅔ cup (165ml) milk*

Peel potatoes, cut in half and boil until cooked through. DO NOT over cook. Drain and place back on the cooktop. Heat the milk separately, once boiled add it to the potatoes and beat 'pointing it to a window' for the best result.

Potatoes Maxim

Serves 4 - 6

- *½ kg smallish potatoes*
- *5 tbs. butter, melted*

Preheat oven 200C. Peel potatoes and place in a bowl, then drizzle with the melted butter. Season with sea salt and pepper and gently mix the potatoes to coat with butter. Arrange the potatoes in a single layer on a baking tray. Place tray in the oven and bake for 30 - 40 minutes, or until the potatoes are cooked and browned.

Optional: Add 1 tbs. cumin to the seasoning.

Rosemary & Thyme Potatoes

Serves 4. These are lovely served with almost anything!

- *4 large potatoes*
- *2 tbs. olive oil*
- *1 tbs. dried or fresh rosemary*
- *1 tbs. thyme*

Preheat oven to 180C. Peel potatoes and halve. On the non-flat side, make 4 or 5 slices across the potatoes, slicing about three-quarters of the way through. Combine potatoes with oil in large baking dish, sprinkle with sea salt and pepper. Bake for approximately 20 - 30 minutes until potatoes are browned and tender. Mix herbs and sprinkle.

Rosemary & Mustard Mashed Potatoes

Serves 4. Kim's family's favourite mash recipe!

- *4 large potatoes*
- *2 tbs. fresh rosemary*
- *1 tbs. Dijon mustard*

Boil ½ cup (125ml) water with rosemary in a small saucepan. Reduce heat and simmer until infused. Boil potatoes, drain and add rosemary liquid. Mash well adding the dijon to taste.

Optional: For a creamier texture add 2 tbs. cream.

Sautéed Lemon Potatoes

Serves 4. A recipe from the very creative Michelle Dodd. These are sensational !!

- *4 medium potatoes*
- *Juice of 1 lemon*
- *3 tbs. extra virgin olive oil*
- *1 tbs. butter*

Peel and cut potatoes into eighths, parboil (boil until half cooked) for 3 minutes. Heat oil, butter and lemon juice in baking dish in a hot oven. Toss in potatoes basting with liquid and cook for 15 - 20 minutes or until golden.

Optional: Add freshly ground garlic to oil and lemon juice.

Simplest Potato Bake Ever

Serves 6. A recipe from Anje ... One word – D.I.V.I.N.E!!

- *6 potatoes*
- *300ml tub of cream*
- *1 pkt French onion soup*

Slice potatoes 5mm thick then place into a baking dish. Combine cream and soup, pour over potatoes and bake in oven 180C for 30 - 40 minutes or until done.

Stuffed Baked Potatoes

Serves 4

- *4 large washed potatoes*
- *320g sour cream*
- *1 cup (100g) cheddar cheese, grated*
- *500g of steamed vegetables (mushrooms, zucchini, peppers, squash)*

Pierce potatoes with a skewer and add to a saucepan ½ full of boiling water. Bring to boil, cover and simmer for 15 minutes, or until just cooked. Steam vegetables of your choice separately for 5 minutes, or until cooked. Drain potatoes and scoop about 2 tbs. of flesh from each potato and discard. Mix sour cream, cheese and vegetables together. Spoon the mixture into the hole and serve hot.

Sweet Potato Chips

Serves 4 as a side dish. Recipe from Cyndi O'Meara.

- *1 orange sweet potato, peeled and sliced*
- *3 tbs. extra virgin olive oil*
- *Sea salt*

Preheat over to 200C. Place sweet potato in a large baking dish, drizzle with oil, coating well. Bake for 40 minutes or until golden brown. Sprinkle with sea salt before serving.

Potato Fritters

- *3 medium potatoes*
- *2 eggs, beaten*
- *½ cup (85g) plain flour*
- *Oil for frying (1 tbs. per fritter for frying)*

Grate potatoes and drain excess juice. Stir in eggs, flour and a pinch of salt. Heat oil in fry pan and add potato mixture in 2 tablespoon batches. Cook for 5 - 10 minutes then turn and cook for another 5 minutes. Drain excess oil on absorbent paper.

Vegetables

Let food be your medicine and medicine be your food

Hippocrates

Asparagus with Butter & Parmesan

Serves 4

- *2 bunches asparagus*
- *1 tbs. butter, melted*
- *½ cup (50g) parmesan cheese, grated*

Bring water to boil in a large frying pan, add asparagus and simmer uncovered for 2 minutes before draining. Serve drizzled with melted butter and cheese. Season with sea salt and pepper.

Asparagus with Balsamic Dressing

Serves 4

- *2 bunches asparagus*
- *4 tbs. extra virgin olive oil*
- *4 tbs. balsamic vinegar*
- *2 vine ripened tomatoes, diced*

Cook asparagus under a grill for 5 minutes or until tender. Serve drizzled with combined oil, vinegar and tomato.

Optional: For extra taste, sprinkle with 2 tbs. finely chopped basil leaves.

Bacon Stuffed Mushrooms

Serves 4

- *4 large field mushrooms*
- *4 rashers bacon*
- *¼ cup (60g) breadcrumbs*
- *½ cup (50g) mozzarella cheese, grated*

Preheat oven to 180C. Remove mushroom stalks. Cut bacon rashers into fine strips and lightly fry. Mix breadcrumbs and cheese together and add bacon. Place mushrooms, top side down, on a paper lined baking tray. Spoon ingredients onto the mushroom and bake for 15 minutes.

Baked Sweet Pumpkin

Serves 4

- *1 small butternut pumpkin (butternut squash)*
- *1 tsp. brown sugar*
- *½ tsp. butter*
- *2 tsp. ground cinnamon*

Preheat oven 190C. Cut top off the pumpkin and scrape out all the seeds. Combine butter and brown sugar and spoon mixture into the pumpkin. Sprinkle with cinnamon and return the lid. Sit pumpkin in a baking pan with 2cm of water in the bottom. Bake for 30 minutes, or until tender.

Baked Rice

Serves 4

- *1 cup rice (185g), uncooked*
- *2 tbs. butter, melted*
- *500ml carton beef stock*
- *½ cup (50g) parmesan cheese, grated*

Preheat oven 180C. Place butter in a casserole dish, add rice and pour beef stock over it. Sprinkle with parmesan and bake for 45 minutes.

Beans with Garlic & Pine Nuts

Serves 4. These are scrumptious!

- *400g beans*
- *3 tbs. olive oil*
- *1 or 2 cloves garlic, halved*
- *4 tbs. pine nuts*

Trim the beans, microwave in enough water to cover for 1 minute then drain. Heat oil and garlic in small frying pan over low heat until garlic just changes colour. Add beans, sauté for a minute then add pine nuts that have been lightly toasted (on a baking tray in 180C oven for 3 minutes), stir until heated through.

Boiled Rice

Serves 4 - 6

- *2 cups (500ml) water*
- *1 cup (185g) rice*

Bring water and rice to boil, stirring occasionally. Lower heat, cover and simmer for 15 - 20 minutes. Remove from heat and stand, covered, for a further 5 minutes. Rinse under hot water and serve.

Optional: Buy the '90 seconds microwave' bags of rice from the supermarket ... Even easier!

Caramelised Roast Pumpkin

Serves 4

- *½ kg butternut pumpkin (butternut squash)*
- *3 tbs. olive oil*

Preheat oven 250C. Leave the skin on the pumpkin or if preferred, remove, discard the seeds and cut the flesh into chunks. Put the oil in a roasting pan and place on a medium heat. When simmering hot, add the pumpkin chunks and season generously with sea salt and pepper. Turn the pumpkin and allow to colour. Place the pan in the oven and roast for 30 - 35 minutes, turning occasionally until pumpkin has a crisp brown surface. Serve immediately or use in salads.

Cheesy Peas

Serves 4

- *500g frozen peas*
- *2½ tbs. butter*
- *1 tbs. lemon juice*
- *½ cup (50g) parmesan cheese, shaved*

Microwave peas, butter and lemon juice on high for 3 minutes. Remove, stir and microwave for a further 2 minutes. Allow to stand covered for 2 - 3 minutes, transfer to serving dish and sprinkle with parmesan. Serve hot.

Crunchy Snow Peas

Serves 4. Thanks Michelle Dodd, for this terrific little tip!

- *400g snow peas*

Top and tail snow peas and place in a sealable container. Boil your jug, cover peas with boiling water and seal for 3 minutes, drain and serve.

Easy Fried Rice

Serves 2. S.c.r.u.m.p.t.i.o.u.s

- *1 cup (185g) brown rice*
- *1 egg*
- *2 rashers bacon*
- *4 tbs. soy sauce*

While rice is boiling, fry the egg, breaking the yolk to ensure spreading. Dice bacon and fry until crisp. Drain rice and rinse under hot water, stirring it to separate. Drain thoroughly and add to bacon and egg, cover evenly with soy sauce.

Optional: Also nice with diced red peppers, pineapple, peas, chopped spring onions & corn and a tsp. or 2 of sweet chilli sauce.

Fluffy Rice Without a Cooker

Serves 4 - 6. Recipe from Cyndi O'Meara.

- *1.25 ltr boiling water*
- *2½ cups (460g) long grain white rice, washed*

Preheat oven to 190C. Place rice in a large glass ovenproof casserole dish with a lid. Add boiling water and stir until smooth. Cover and cook in oven for 30 minutes.

Fried Brussels Sprouts

Serves 4

- *12 Brussels sprouts*
- *4 rashers bacon*
- *1 tbs. walnut oil*

Cut a criss-cross into the base of the sprouts. Boil approx. 8 - 10 minutes or until until cooked. Dice bacon and then fry until crisp, fold through the cooked sprouts with oil and sauté for 2 minutes.

Garlic Mushrooms

Serves 4

- *500g mushrooms*
- *2 tbs. extra virgin olive oil*
- *1 or 2 cloves garlic, crushed*
- *¼ cup freshly chopped flat-leaf parsley*

Preheat oven 180C. Place mushrooms in a large baking dish, drizzle with oil and garlic, roast in oven 15 minutes or until mushrooms are tender and browned lightly. Stir in parsley.

Tip: Cook close to serving.

Honey Carrots

Serves 4 - 6

- *1 bunch baby carrots*
- *½ cup (125ml) water*
- *1 tbs. manuka honey*
- *2 tsp. butter*

Boil water in a saucepan. Place the carrots in water and return to the boil, simmer for 10 minutes. Drain, add honey and butter and toss well.

Optional: Sprinkle with sesame seeds at Christmas time for presentation.

Honey & Mustard Roast Parsnips

- *1kg parsnips, quartered*
- *4 tbs. extra virgin olive oil*
- *3 tbs. honey*
- *4 tbs. wholegrain mustard*

Preheat the oven to 200C. Bring the parsnips to the boil in lightly salted water and simmer for 5 minutes. Heat the oil in a large roasting tin until smoking. Drain the parsnips and add to the oil. Coat well and roast for 40 minutes until crispy. Mix the honey and mustard and pour over the parsnips, then cook for a further 5 minutes.

Honey Soy Noodles

Serves 4

- *500g pkt Hokkien noodles*
- *1 tbs. sesame oil*
- *2 tbs. tamari soy sauce*
- *2 tbs. manuka honey*

Soften noodles in a bowl filled with hot water, drain and set aside. Combine oil, soy sauce and honey together. Heat a wok to medium temperature and add liquid mixture, quickly add noodles and stir continuously for about 3 minutes.

Optional: This dish is delicious with some cubed and stir fried chicken or Tofu and a variety of vegetables.

Lemon Broccoli

Serves 4 - 6. Recipe from Cyndi O'Meara.

- *1 tbs. fresh lemon juice*
- *1 head broccoli cut into medium sized florets*

Bring 1 cup water to the boil in a medium saucepan. Add broccoli, return to the boil and simmer for 3 minutes. Remove from heat and drain. Drizzle with lemon juice before serving.

Minted Pea Mash

Serves 4. Great with steak.

- *500g Charlotte potatoes, peeled and chopped*
- *500g frozen peas*
- *⅓ cup (80ml) milk*
- *4 stems fresh mint leaves, chopped*

Cook potatoes in a large saucepan of boiling water until soft. Add peas and cook for 5 minutes. Drain and cool slightly. Return peas and potatoes to pan, add milk and mash until almost smooth, mix through mint leaves. Season well with salt and pepper.

Mushy Peas

Serves 4

- *200g pkt dried peas*
- *2 tsp.baking soda*

Soak dried peas overnight in a large bowl in 3 cups of water (750ml) and baking soda. The baking soda is important as that is what makes the peas break down. The next day, drain the peas, add enough water just to cover, and simmer for 20 minutes. The peas will break up nicely without mashing. Add a little water if needed to bring to the consistency you like. Don't season until the end or it toughens the peas.

Optional: Serve with malt vinegar or mint if desired.

Oven Baked Tomatoes

Serves 3

- *3 vine ripened tomatoes*
- *3 tsp. basil pesto*
- *3 tbs. grated parmesan cheese*

Cut the tomatoes in half. Place in an ovenproof dish, cut side up. Season each with sea salt and pepper. Smooth pesto over each and top with parmesan. Bake in a preheated 200C oven for 20 minutes.

Queensland Battered Vegetables

Serves 2. An Aussie favourite from Paul Bermingham.

- *1 cup (125g) plain organic flour*
- *375ml bottle of beer*
- *1 ltr. extra virgin olive oil*
- *2 cups vegetables (mushrooms, sweet potatoes, peppers, zucchini, carrots, squash, whole beans, cauliflower, broccoli, parsnips, all cut into bite-sized pieces)*

Combine flour and beer in a big bowl and mix to make a thick, creamy batter. Generously dip and coat all vegetables in batter. Heat oil in a medium size saucepan. Fry vegetables till batter is golden brown. Remove, drain and lay on a paper towel to absorb extra oil. Serve warm.

Optional: Serve with aioli.

Roast Beetroot

- *1 bunch whole beetroot*

Wash the beets well and trim the leaves leaving about 2cm of stalk. Remove most of the root, but not all. Do not peel. Wrap well in foil and bake in 180C oven for 40 minutes or until tender. Unwrap and peel.

Optional: Serve with grilled salmon, black pepper and butter or horseradish cream ... mmmmm!

Roasted Corn with Parmesan & Cayenne

Serves 4

- *4 fresh cobs of corn*
- *2 tbs. whole egg mayonnaise*
- *2 tbs. grated parmesan cheese*
- *½ tsp. cayenne pepper*

Preheat oven 180C. Place the corn, in its husks, directly on the oven rack and roast for 20 minutes until the corn is soft when you press on it. To finish, peel the husks, remove the corn silk, and tie the husks in a knot so you can hold on to it like a handle. Char the corn on a hot grill, or under a grill, until the kernels are slightly blackened all around and start popping (about 6 minutes). Rub the corn with mayonnaise, sprinkle with parmesan and cayenne pepper, ensure well coated.

Optional: Serve with lime wedges.

Sautéed Asparagus

Serves 4

- *2 bunches asparagus*
- *4 tbs. extra virgin olive oil*

Heat heavy based fry pan, douse with olive oil. Reduce heat and sauté asparagus until cooked, season lightly with sea salt and pepper.

Seasoned Roasted Vegetables

Serves 2

- *1 cup (250ml) extra virgin olive oil*
- *1½ tsp. oregano powder*
- *500g of veges of choice (whole mushrooms, diced sweet potatoes, red pepper cut into 4 with seeds removed, topped and tailed zucchini, carrots sliced down the middle and halved, squash sliced in half, whole beans, onions halved, etc.)*

Preheat oven to 180C. Place vegetables on a baking tray. Coat with oil and bake until cooked. Remove from tray and place onto a serving plate. Combine 1 tsp. sea salt and oregano and sprinkle over vegetables.

Snow Peas in Garlic Mint Butter

Serves 8

- *200g snow peas*
- *1½ tbs. butter*
- *2 cloves garlic, crushed*
- *2 sprigs mint, chopped*

Top and tail snow peas. Melt butter in a frying pan, then add garlic and mint. Stir in peas, sauté until just tender.

Steamed Broccoli scattered with Pine Nuts

Serves 4

- *1 head of broccoli*
- *1 tbs. butter*
- *4 tbs. toasted pine nuts*

Separate florets of broccoli and steam until just tender and still bright green. Place into serving dish, dot with butter, scatter with pine nuts and black pepper the lot.

Stuffed Pepper

Makes 6

- *500g premium mince*
- *6 red pepper*
- *1 medium onion*

Preheat oven to 150C. Scrape out pepper. Cook the mince and onion season generously with pepper and a little sea salt. Spoon into red pepper. Bake for ½ an hour on a paper lined baking tray.

Optional: Stuff with leftover couscous mixed with the zest of a lemon.

Zucchini Hash Browns

Makes 4

- *1 zucchini (courgette), grated*
- *2 tbs. extra virgin olive oil*
- *2 eggs, beaten slightly*
- *Organic mixed seasoning to taste*

Heat oil in a heavy pan. Mix all ingredients together in a medium size bowl and gently drop 1 tbs. of mixture in hot oil. When brown on one side, turn and cook on the other side. Stack on a plate and keep warm until the whole batch is cooked.

Optional: Top with sweet chilli sauce, sour cream or butter.

Mains

The opinions expressed by the man of this house are not necessarily those of the management!

A wife!!!

Beef

4 Ingredient Chilli

Serves 4

- *450g lean mince*
- *1 pkt. chilli seasoning mix*
- *400g can chilli beans in sauce*
- *500ml tomato juice*

Brown mince and drain fat. Combine beef and remaining ingredients in a large pot. Bring to boil then simmer uncovered for 30 - 40 minutes or until desired thickness.

Optional: Serve with rice and sprinkle with grated cheese if desired.

Beef Patties

Serves 4. A recipe from Rebecca Butler.

- *500g lean mince*
- *2 large potatoes, mashed*
- *½ onion, finely chopped*
- *3 tbs. extra virgin olive oil*

Mix mince, potatoes and onions in a bowl, season with sea salt and pepper. Once combined, roll into patties. Heat oil in frying pan and depending on thickness cook, turning occasionally, until a crusty brown exterior forms all over.

Optional: Serve with gravy and vegetables.

Beef Stir-Fry

Serves 4

- *500g stir-fry beef*
- *⅔ cup (165ml) barbequed stir-fry sauce (see Sauces)*
- *2 tbs. sesame oil*
- *4 - 6 spring onions, chopped*

Mix stir-fry sauce and meat together, allow to stand for 15 minutes. Heat oil in a wok or frying pan. Stir-fry meat in batches for 1 minute, or until cooked on the outside and medium on the inside. Trim the spring onions and cut into thin lengthwise strips. Quickly stir-fry in wok. Serve meat on top of a salad (even just shredded ice-berg lettuce is nice) and top with spring onions and jus.

Optional: This is delicious using just plain BBQ sauce if you don't have barbequed stir-fry sauce.

Beef Stock

A recipe from Jan Neale.

- *1 kg beef soup bones*
- *1 bouquet garni*
- *2 onions, chopped coarsely*
- *1 cup of mixed vegetables (carrot, celery, peppers etc whatever is available)*

Place all ingredients in saucepan, cover with water and boil. Reduce heat and simmer until meat is falling from the bones. Strip bones and discard. For a clear stock, strain.

Optional: Retain meat and vegetables to use in a casserole or curry.

Beef Stroganoff

Serves 4. Another beauty from Jan Neale.

- *500g beef strips*
- *250g mushrooms, coarsely chopped*
- *1 pkt beef stroganoff seasoning*
- *320g sour cream*

Heat a non-stick frying pan and lightly fry beef strips.
Add mushrooms, sour cream and stroganoff mix, stir well.
Add water to achieve your required consistency.

Beef Wellington

Serves 6. A recipe from Wendy Beattie. This is a divine dinner party main.

- *2½ sheets puff pastry*
- *1¼ kg fillet beef*
- *250g pepper pate*
- *200g mushrooms, sliced*

Remove all fat from meat. Tie securely with string to hold shape. Grind black pepper over meat and press firmly. Heat a non-stick frying pan and sear meat until golden on all sides. Place meat on baking tray and put in 180C oven for 10 minutes. Remove and allow to completely cool. Remove string. Beat pate until soft and spread a thin layer over meat. Sprinkle with sea salt. Press thinly sliced mushrooms into pate. Wrap fillet in puff pastry, making sure it is totally sealed. Decorate top with strips of pastry and bake in a 250C oven for 5 minutes. Reduce heat to 180C and bake for a further 30 - 40 minutes.

Optional: Brush pastry with beaten egg for a really presentable finish.

Chilli Con Carne

Serves 4

- *500g lean mince*
- *1 pkt chilli con carne seasoning*
- *400g can tomatoes*
- *300g can red kidney beans*

Brown mince in non-stick frying pan. Add chilli con carne mix. Add tomatoes, red kidney beans and ½ cup of water and stir well. Cover and simmer gently for 15 minutes, or until mince is cooked, stirring regularly.

Optional: We often add whatever other vegetables we have in the fridge; onions, carrots, peppers, etc.

Coffee & Pepper Crusted Steaks

Serves 4. This is charmingly unusual!

- *4 steaks, 2 - 3cm thick*
- *2 tbs. whole coffee beans*
- *2 tbs. whole black peppercorns*
- *1 tbs. extra virgin olive oil for brushing steaks*

Coarsely grind the coffee beans and peppercorns. Press the mixture evenly on both sides of the steaks. Spray steaks lightly with oil, then grill or barbecue the steaks over direct high heat for 8 - 10 minutes, turning once halfway through grilling time (do not turn steaks until you see beads of juice on the surface). Remove the steaks from the grill and season both sides with sea salt. Allow to rest for 3 minutes before serving.

Creamy Meatballs

Serves 4 - 6

- *750g lean mince*
- *250g sour cream*
- *1 tsp. garlic salt*
- *1 tbs. extra virgin olive oil*

Combine first 3 ingredients. Roll into patties. Allow oil to heat in a frying pan and then fry patties over a medium heat.

Optional: Roll in breadcrumbs before frying.

Easy Roast Beef

Serves 4-6. A recipe from Shane McCosker. This is a sensational Sunday roast and soooooooooo easy!

- *1 kg beef rib roast*
- *1 pkt French onion soup mix*
- *400g tin cream of mushroom soup*

Preheat oven to 180C. Place a large sheet of alfoil in a baking pan, enough to fully wrap the beef. Place beef in the centre of the foil and bring foil up to make a bowl. Combine soups in a bowl. Mix thoroughly and pour over beef. Fold alfoil to seal tightly. Bake for 1 hour or until tender, serve with delicious gravy in the bottom of the bag.

Optional: Serve with roast vegetables.

Glen's Corned Beef

Serves 6. A recipe perfected by Glen, Kim's husband.

- *1 kg silverside beef*
- *1ltr. ginger ale*

Place meat in large pot, add the ginger ale and cook for 1 hour or until tender.

Optional: Serve with vegetables and horseradish sauce.

Kim's Corned Beef

Serves 6

- *1 kg silverside beef*
- *10 cloves*
- *4 tbs. maple syrup*
- *Black pepper*

Place meat in a large pot, cover with water. Bring to boil, reduce heat and cook for 1 hour or until tender. When cooked place meat in a shallow baking dish, press cloves into meat, drizzle with syrup and dust with freshly cracked pepper. Place in preheated 180C oven to glaze for 15 minutes ... *Yum!*

Massaman Curry

Serves 4. Served up in the Bermingham household regularly!

- *500g lean beef strips*
- *1 tbs. Massaman curry paste*
- *3 Desiree potatoes, peeled and cubed*
- *400ml coconut milk*

Place beef with ¼ cup of water in a non stick frypan or large saucepan and cook on high heat till browned on the outside. Combine massaman curry and coconut cream and add to beef. Add potatoes and turn down to very lowest heat and simmer for 30 minutes or until potatoes are cooked through.

Optional: Can add ½ cup (60g) of cashews and serve with rice.

Pan-Fried Steak

Serves 2. Ever wondered how to cook steaks well?

- *2 x 200g fillet steaks*
- *2 tbs. extra virgin olive oil*

Preheat heavy frying pan until hot. Add oil and reduce heat by a quarter. Place steak in pan and cook for 8 minutes for medium doneness (season with sea salt and pepper ½ way through this), turn once only, then cook until desired doneness is achieved. Take fillet off heat and let it rest for 4 - 5 minutes.

Pesto Stuffed Steaks

Serves 4. F.a.s.t & F.a.b.u.l.o.u.s

- *2 rib eye steaks (about 3cm thick)*
- *¼ cup (65g) basil pesto*
- *3 tbs. grated parmesan cheese*
- *1 tbs. extra virgin olive oil*

Preheat heavy frying pan until hot. Cut into the side of each steak (minimising the width of the opening cut), forming a deep pocket (do not cut through). Mix pesto and cheese and spread into pockets. Press closed and drizzle with oil. Place steaks carefully in the pan and cook for 10 minutes for medium doneness, turn once when you see juices on the surface of the steak. When done, remove, cover and let stand for 5 minutes. Cut beef into thick strips to serve.

Pot Pie

Serves 2 and is the perfect meal to serve up while watching the footy!

- *500g lean mince*
- *250g fruit chutney*
- *½ onion peeled and chopped finely*
- *½ sheet of butter puff pastry*

Preheat oven to 185C. Place onion in a non stick fry pan with ½ cup of water and cook on medium heat for 5 minutes. Add mince and cook till brown, then add the chutney. Stir through till warm and spoon mixture into 2 pie sized ramekins. Cut 2 ramekin sized circles out of the puff pastry and top pie with each. Bake in oven for 15 minutes or until pastry top is golden.

Optional: Substitute fruit chutney for tomato chutney for a change.

Quick Meatloaf

Serves 4

- *500g lean organic mince*
- *3 free-range eggs, lightly beaten*
- *¾ cup (90g) organic breadcrumbs*
- *¼ cup (65g) tomato paste (reserve a tbs.)*

Preheat oven to 180C. Mix all ingredients together and place in a lined rectangular baking dish. Spread reserved tomato paste on top of meatloaf. Bake for 50 minutes or until lightly browned on top. Serve hot with vegetables, salad or mash potato. This is also great to freeze.

Tip: For a Mexican meatloaf substitute tomato paste with a 270g jar of picante (hot) sauce. Use ⅔ in the loaf and ⅓ to coat. Reduce eggs to 2.

Optional: For an added zing add 1 tsp. of curry powder. To get your 5 vegetable quota for the day, add shredded carrot, sweet potato, diced mushrooms, peas and corn to the mix before baking.

Rissoles

Makes 8. From playgroup chef extraordinaire, Aine Watkins!

- *500g lean mince*
- *2 medium onions, diced*
- *2 medium eggs*
- *2 tbs. flour*

Preheat a sandwich press machine. Mix all ingredients, except for 1 tbs. flour. Divide into 8 even amounts and roll into balls, dust with remaining flour. Place in between the sandwich press plates and cook till done.

Roast Beef with Horseradish Cream

Serves 4

- *1kg beef rib roast*
- *1 tbs. mixed sea salt and pepper*
- *½ tsp. dried thyme*
- *Horseradish cream (see sauces)*

Heat oven to 150C. Rub the roast with salt, pepper and thyme. Arrange roast in large shallow roasting pan. Roast about 2 hours in the lower third of your oven. Transfer roast to a carving board and cover loosely with alfoil. Let stand 15 minutes. Carve and serve with horseradish cream.

Optional: To quicken cooking time, increase heat to 180C and check after 1 hour.

Salsa Patties

Serves 4 - 6. A recipe from the beautiful Rebecca Butler.

- *750g lean mince*
- *⅓ cup (90g) salsa*
- *22 crushed Ritz crackers*
- *2 tbs. olive oil*

Combine, mince, salsa and crackers. Roll into 6 patties. Heat frying pan, add oil and brown patties on both sides before serving.

Optional: Delicious served with rice, salad and a dollop of guacamole.

Veal Casserole

Serves 4. This is (was) a third generation Kellow family secret!

- *500g diced veal*
- *200g diced bacon*
- *2 celery stalks, washed and sliced*
- *400g tin cream of chicken soup*

Pour all ingredients into a casserole dish. Place in a moderate oven and bake at 160C for 2 hours.

Chicken

The more we share, the more we have

Someone wise

Apricot Chicken

Serves 4. A recipe from Jennette McCosker.

- *8 chicken pieces*
- *500g can apricot nectar*
- *1 pkt French onion soup*
- *1 brown onion, diced*

Place chicken pieces in a casserole dish with soup and onion and season with sea salt and pepper. Add apricot nectar and stir. Cover and bake in 180C oven for 1½ hrs.

Optional: For a change, place chicken in a plastic bag and coat in flour, salt and pepper and lightly fry. Follow cooking instructions as above but cook for 1 hour.

Butter Chicken

Serves 2. A favourite Bermingham recipe, easy and quick!

- *4 chicken breasts*
- *4 tbs. butter chicken seasoning*
- *500ml cream*
- *1½ tbs. butter*

Preheat oven to 200C. Mix butter chicken seasoning with 1½ cups of hot water and spread over chicken breasts. Marinate in mixture for at least an hour in the fridge. Melt butter in a non stick fry pan on medium heat, add chicken and cook for about 8 minutes or until cooked through. Turn heat down to a low heat and add the cream, stirring through. Serve warm.

Optional: Serve with beans over fluffy rice (see vegetables).

Cajun Chicken Kebabs

Serves 1. Light and luscious with a simple salad!

- *140g chicken breast fillet, cubed*
- *½ red pepper*
- *½ brown onion*
- *2 tsp. cajun seasoning*

Preheat grill on high. Thread cubes of chicken, red pepper and onion onto skewers (soak in water first). Sprinkle with seasoning then grill for 2 minutes each side or until cooked.

Cheese & Prosciutto Chicken

Serves 4. Another great recipe from Wendy Beattie's vibrant kitchen.

- *4 chicken fillet breasts*
- *4 slices Swiss cheese*
- *8 slices prosciutto*
- *2 tbs. extra virgin olive oil*

Preheat oven 200C. Cut lengthways through each fillet to make a pocket (keeping the width of the initial incision smallish), leaving 1 cm at each end. Stuff each fillet with cheese and prosciutto. Heat oil in large frying pan over med/high heat. Add chicken breasts and cook for 1 - 2 minutes until golden on each side. Transfer to baking tray and roast for 7 - 10 minutes or until just cooked through. Cover and set aside to rest for 5 minutes.

Optional: Serve with sweet potato mash and baby spinach.

Chicken & Jarlsberg Casserole

Serves 6. A recipe from the Australian Olympian Julie McDonald OAM. This is GLORIOUS on chilly winter's nights!

- *6 chicken fillet breasts*
- *6 slices jarlsberg cheese*
- *400g tin cream of chicken soup*
- *¼ cup (60ml) milk*

Preheat oven 150C. Place chicken in a casserole dish and cover with cheese. Mix well soup and milk and pour over chicken. Bake for an hour, uncovered.

Chicken Marsala

Serves 2

- *4 chicken breasts*
- *200g sliced fresh mushrooms*
- *½ cup (125ml) Marsala wine*
- *¾ cup (185ml) cream*

Flatten the chicken a little. Sauté chicken in a large non stick skillet or fry pan for 15 – 20 minutes or until cooked through and juices run clear. Add mushrooms and sauté until soft. Add Marsala wine and bring to boil. Boil for 2 – 4 minutes seasoning with salt and pepper to taste if you like. Stir in the cream and simmer until heated through, about 5 minutes.

Optional: Serve with vegetables.

Chicken Pie

Serves 4 - 6. This re-defines fast & fabulous!

- *2 sheets puff pastry*
- *400g can condensed cream of chicken soup*
- *½ cooked chicken without skin, cubed*
- *500g frozen mixed veges, thawed*

Preheat oven 180C. Line a non-stick pie dish with first sheet of pastry. Combine remaining ingredients in a bowl, season with sea salt and pepper and pour into pastry. Cover with remaining sheet, seal edges well by pressing with a fork. Cut several slits in the pie lid and bake for 30 minutes, or until lid is golden brown.

Optional: Brush with beaten egg or milk for a very presentable finish.

Chicken, Pumpkin & Chickpea Curry

Serves 6

- *700g piece pumpkin*
- *8 boneless, skinless chicken thighs*
- *300g can chickpeas*
- *420g jar Korma curry sauce*

De-seed pumpkin, wrap in cling film and microwave on high for 5 minutes or until almost cooked. Peel and cut into cubes. Cut chicken thighs in half. Drain chickpeas. Place chicken, pumpkin, chickpeas and curry sauce in a saucepan. Wash jar with about ¼ cup of hot water and add to saucepan. Cover and cook on medium for about 30 minutes.

Optional: Serve with steamed rice and garnish with fresh coriander.

Chicken Stir-Fry

Serves 2. This is effortless and so tasty!!

- *300g chicken breast fillets*
- *3 tbs. sweet chilli sauce*
- *3 tbs. hoisin sauce*
- *3 tbs. soy sauce*

Slice the chicken breast into thin slices. Line electric frying pan with baking paper and heat on high. Add sweet chilli, hoisin and soy sauce and stir well. When the sauce begins to bubble, add the chicken fillets and stir to combine. Cook until the chicken is done (approximately 5 minutes).

Optional: Add whatever vegetables available, sauté and serve with rice.

Chicken Schnitzel

Serves 4. A family favourite!

- *4 chicken schnitzels*
- *4 tbs. extra virgin olive oil*
- *1 cup (250g) Napolitana sauce*
- *100g mozzarella cheese, grated*

Heat frying pan and add oil. When hot, lightly fry chicken schnitzels. When golden brown on both sides, place on paper lined baking tray. Top evenly with sauce and mozzarella cheese and grill slowly until cheese is bubbling and golden.

Chicken Tikka Masala

Serves 4

- *3 chicken breasts, cut into chunks*
- *2 tbs. Tikka Masala paste*
- *400g tin cream of tomato soup*
- *150ml natural yoghurt*

Heat a non stick fry pan add the chicken and fry for 5 - 6 minutes or until browned. Add the curry paste and soup and simmer for 15 minutes, then stir in the yoghurt and heat through.

Optional: Serve with rice.

Chutney Chicken Dish

Serves 2. This is deliciously simple!

- *2 chicken breasts*
- *2 tbs. fruit chutney*
- *2 tbs. French mustard*
- *¼ cup (25g) grated cheddar cheese*

Mix the chutney with the mustard and cover the chicken breasts. Put chicken breasts in a baking dish, cover with grated cheese and place in oven for 15 - 20 minutes at 180C.

Optional: Serve with rice or vegetables.

Curried Chicken

Serves 4. So easy and yummy!

- *1kg raw chicken pieces*
- *1 tbs. curry powder*
- *410g tin evaporated milk*
- *400g tin cream of mushroom soup*

Preheat oven to 180C. Cut chicken into bight size pieces and place into an ovenproof dish. Mix all other ingredients together and pour over chicken and bake for one hour.

Green Chicken Curry

Serves 4. A yummy recipe from Shane McCosker.

- *4 chicken thighs, skinless*
- *1 cup green beans, cut into 5 cm pieces*
- *¼ cup green curry paste*
- *400ml coconut cream*

Cut chicken into strips. Heat wok or large frying pan; add green curry paste, cooking and stirring for a minute or so or until fragrant. Add chicken and cook, stirring for about 10 minutes or until almost done. Stir in coconut cream and bring to boil. Simmer uncovered for 30 minutes. Add beans and simmer for further 10 minutes, or until just tender.

Optional: We often add more vegetables.

Grilled Chicken with Roasted Peppers & Tomato Sauce

Serves 4

- *4 red peppers*
- *8 skinless chicken drumsticks*
- *¼ cup (65g) sun-dried tomato pesto*
- *1 large tomato*

Cut peppers in half, de-seed and place cut side down under grill. Place chicken under grill also and grill until peppers skin starts to blister. Remove peppers and continue to cook chicken until juices run clear, 15 - 20 minutes. Remove skin and blend with pesto until smooth. Cut tomato in half, de-seed and chop into small cubes. Serve chicken with roasted peppers and tomato sauce, topped with cubed tomato.

Honey Baked Chicken

Serves 4 - 6

- *1 pkt French onion soup*
- *¾ cup white wine*
- *3 tbs. honey*
- *1 kg chicken pieces*

Combine French onion soup, honey and white wine and pour evenly over chicken pieces in a shallow ovenproof dish. Cover and bake at 180C for 1 hour. Remove cover, reduce heat to 150C and bake for a further 30 minutes.

Honey Mustard Chicken Breasts

Serves 4

- *4 chicken breast fillets*
- *¼ cup (80g) honey*
- *2 tbs. Dijon mustard*

Pound the chicken breast fillets. Mix the honey and mustard and spread over the chicken leaving a little for basting. Grill for 15 - 20 minutes, turning and basting until done.

Indian Chicken Curry

Makes 4. Very easy and very yummy!

- *1 roast chicken*
- *225g natural yoghurt*
- *6 tbs. mayonnaise*
- *2 tbs. curry powder*

Chop roast chicken into bite-size pieces. In a bowl mix together yoghurt, mayo and curry powder. Marinate chicken pieces in yoghurt mixture for at least 1 hour then bake in a moderate oven until heated through.

Optional: Serve with rice, fresh coriander and lemon wedges.

Kazza's Wonderful Chicken

Serves 2. A recipe from Karyn Turnbull-Markus.

- *2 chicken breast fillets, thickly sliced*
- *½ cup (160g) sour cream*
- *¼ cup (40g) slivered almonds*
- *½ cup (50g) grated Jarslberg cheese*

Dip breasts into sour cream, mix almonds and jarslberg together and then roll chicken in this, coat well. Place in a shallow oven dish and bake at 160C for about 20 minutes, or until chicken is golden brown.

Korma Chicken

Serves 4

- *3 chicken breasts, cut into stir-fry pieces*
- *350g Korma, mildly spiced organic sauce*
- *2 carrots, peeled and julienned*
- *Freshly chopped coriander*

Into a warm frying pan add 3 tbs water, seal chicken on all sides. Add sauce and reduce heat. Whilst simmering, place carrot sticks into microwave safe dish, cover with water and microwave for 2 minutes or until just done. Add to sauce and continue to simmer for 5 minutes. Serve over rice, topped generously with fresh coriander ... *Healthy and colourful!*

Mascarpone & Coriander Chicken

Serves 4. A super recipe from the talented Janelle McCosker.

- *6 chicken thigh fillets*
- *4 tbs. mascarpone*
- *½ bunch roughly chopped coriander*
- *1 tbs. extra virgin olive oil*

Quarter each chicken thigh. Heat oil in a frying pan, add chicken and cook until golden, turning occasionally. Reduce heat and add mascarpone, stir until melted, simmering until mascarpone begins to bubble. Add coriander and mix, remove from heat and season with sea salt and pepper.

Optional: Delicious served with a fresh Asian salad.

Pesto Chicken

Serves 2

- *4 chicken breast halves*
- *1 tbs. olive oil*
- *3 tbs. basil pesto*
- *8 thin slices mozzarella cheese*

Pound chicken breasts to flatten slightly. Heat oil in non stick fry pan and add chicken and sauté over medium to high heat until browned on both sides (about 10 minutes). Divide pesto between chicken breasts spreading almost to the edge. Top with cheese slices and heat just until the cheese is melted. Serve with veges.

Pesto & Chicken Parcels

Serves 4. A recipe from Kelly Mauger.

- *4 chicken thighs*
- *4 tbs. basil pesto*
- *125g camembert cheese*
- *2 sheets puffed pastry*

Preheat oven 180C. Rub one side of the chicken thigh with pesto and season with sea salt and pepper. Cut camembert into thin strips and cover chicken.   Start from one end of the chicken thigh and roll it up. Place a sheet of the puffed pastry flat and cut diagonally, place the chicken in the middle and fold to cover sealing the edges with a fork. Bake for 30 minutes.

Polynesian Chicken

Serves 4

- *4 chicken breasts*
- *2 tbs. walnut oil*
- *432g can crushed pineapple, drained*
- *250g jar peach or apricot preserves*

Preheat oven 180C. Arrange chicken breasts in an ovenproof dish. Coat breasts in oil thoroughly and bake uncovered for 15 minutes. Turn chicken over and bake for a further 15 minutes or until tender. Drain pan juices. Mix pineapple and preserves together. Pour over chicken and bake for another 15 minutes, or until hot and bubbly.

Sweet & Spicy Chicken

Serves 2

- *6 chicken legs*
- *½ cup (160g) orange marmalade*
- *1 - 2 tsp. chilli powder*

Preheat oven to 180C. Combine marmalade and chilli powder in a plastic sandwich bag, add chicken legs and shake until evenly coated. Place chicken on paper lined baking tray and spoon on any remaining mix. Bake for 30 minutes or until done.

Tomato Flavoured Chicken Legs

Serves 4 - 6. A recipe from the lovely Verna Day.

* *1 kg chicken legs*
* *400g can tomato soup*
* *1 pkt French onion soup*

Preheat oven to 180C. Place chicken legs in an ovenproof dish. Combine tomato soup, French onion mix and ½ cup water then pour over chicken legs. Bake for 1 hour.

Zingy Chicken

Serves 4

* *4 chicken breasts*
* *1 egg, beaten*
* *¼ cup (60ml) soy sauce*
* *1 cup (80g) cornflakes, crushed*

Cut chicken in to thickish strips. Combine egg and soy sauce and dip chicken pieces into it. Coat with crushed cornflakes, place on a paper lined baking tray and cook at 180C for 30 minutes or until done.

Fish

Great love and great achievements involve great risks

Anonymous

Baked Fish

Serves 2

- *2 fresh white fish fillets*
- *1 tsp. butter*
- *1 lemon, sliced*

Coat fish with melted butter and season with sea salt and pepper. Place lemon slices on fish. Wrap fish in alfoil. Cook in 180C oven for 15 - 20 minutes or until tender.

Baked Salmon with Pesto Crust

Serves 4. A recipe from Michelle Dodd. *THIS IS SENSATIONAL!*

- *4 salmon steaks*
- *190g jar basil pesto*
- *100g pecorino cheese, finely grated*
- *1 lemon*

Sear salmon steaks on each side for 2 minutes, skin side down first. Meanwhile combine ½ jar of pesto and all the cheese. Spread this mixture over salmon steaks and squeeze fresh lemon juice over the top. Bake in a moderate oven for 15 minutes.

Optional: Substitute pecorino for parmesan, use extra pesto if required.

Caesar's Fish

Serves 2

- *2 fresh white fish fillets*
- *½ cup (125ml) Caesar salad dressing*
- *1 cup (80g) cornflakes, crushed*
- *½ cup (50g) cheddar cheese, grated*

Preheat oven 160C. Arrange fillets in a single layer on a paper lined baking dish. Drizzle fillets with dressing. Sprinkle cornflakes over the top. Bake for 10 minutes. Top with cheese and bake for an additional 5 minutes, or until fish easily flakes with a fork and cheese is golden brown.

Creamy Basil Fish

Serves 4

- *4 fresh white fish fillets*
- *3 stems fresh basil leaves torn*
- *1 tbs. lemon juice*
- *4 tbs. sour cream*

Grill fish under a hot grill for about 3 minutes each side, until cooked. Place basil, juice and cream in a small saucepan and heat slowly, do not boil. Serve over fish.

Optional: This is magic served with sautéed lemon potatoes and fresh salad.

Curried Fish with Coconut Rice

Serves 4. This is a great way to make rice for a change!

- *4 fresh white fish fillets*
- *350g Korma mildly spiced organic sauce*
- *400g can coconut milk*
- *1 cup (185g) jasmine rice*

Cut fish into 2cm cubes. Place in a saucepan with curry sauce.
Bring to the boil and simmer for 5 minutes or until fish is cooked.
Bring ½ cup water and coconut milk to the boil. Add rice and cook
for 12 - 15 minutes or until rice is tender and liquid absorbed. Pile
rice onto four individual serving plates. Top with fish mixture.

Optional: Garnish with fresh coriander.

Dill Prawns

Serves 4

- *4 cloves garlic, sliced*
- *500g prawns, peeled and de-veined*
- *2 tbs. butter*
- *½ tsp. dried dill*

In a small frying pan, melt butter. Add garlic and cook over low
heat until garlic begins to turn light brown. Discard garlic and add
dill. Add prawns and stir over medium heat for about 3 - 4 minutes.
Serve over rice.

Filo Fish

Serves 4. This is so versatile, if you're all fished out, try replacing the fish and tomato sauce with chicken, mango and cheese – yum!

- *8 sheets filo pastry*
- *2 tbs. extra virgin olive oil*
- *4 fresh white fish fillets*
- *1 cup (250ml) tomato sauce*

Preheat oven 200C. Brush a sheet of filo pastry with some olive oil and lay a second sheet on top. Place a piece of fish (or chicken) at the bottom of the pastry and spoon on some tomato sauce (or a couple of slices of mango and some cheese) and roll over tucking in pastry sides to make a neat and closed pastry parcel. Lay parcels on a baking paper lined tray and brush the top of each with more olive oil before baking for 12 minutes or until golden brown.

Fish Fillets with Orange Sauce

Serves 4

- *4 fresh white fish fillets*
- *1 orange*
- *2 tbs. dry white wine*
- *3 tbs. butter*

Place 1 tbs. butter in heavy frying pan and heat. Place fish in pan. Blend 2 tbs. orange juice and wine with remaining 2 tbs. melted butter, pour half over the fish fillets. Sprinkle with sea salt, pepper and 2 tbs. orange zest. Cook for 2 minutes before pouring remaining sauce over fish and continue cooking until fish is done.

Tip: Fish should flake easily with a fork.

Fish with Black Bean Sauce

Serves 4

- 4 tbs. black bean and garlic sauce
- 1 tbs. sesame oil
- 4 fish steaks
- 4 tbs. sesame seeds

Mix black bean and garlic sauce and oil together. Coat fish steaks. Sprinkle with sesame seeds and grill for 4 minutes each side, or until fish is cooked.

Fish Pie

Serves 4. A McCosker household staple ... *Yummy!*

- 350g organic tomato and basil pasta sauce
- 4 white fish fillets, cut into chunks
- 6 Charlotte potatoes
- 1 cup (100g) grated cheddar cheese

Over medium heat pour sauce into a frying pan. Allow to warm, then add fish, cook for 8 minutes or until fish is done. Remove from heat and allow to sit before pouring into a baking dish. Meanwhile peel, cut, boil and mash potatoes. Spread over fish mixture and sprinkle generously with cheese. Grill until cheese has melted and turned a lovely golden colour.

Optional: This is delicious served with a variety of fresh steamed veges.

Garlic Cream King Prawns

Serves 4. A simple classic from Aine Watkins that'll make a Chef of anyone!

- *16 raw king prawns, peeled and de-veined*
- *½ cup (125ml) cream*
- *1 tbs. freshly crushed garlic*
- *2 cups rice*

Boil rice, then rinse under hot water. Meanwhile, place garlic and cream in a wok or fry pan and reduce. Add prawns and cook for 2 minutes or until prawns have turned orange in colour. Serve on a bed of rice.

Ginger Prawns

Serves 4

- *1 clove garlic*
- *500g prawns, peeled and de-veined*
- *2 tsp. minced garlic*
- *1 tbs. lemon juice*

Crush, peel and finely chop garlic. Sauté garlic and ginger in a non-stick fry pan for 2 minutes (may need a little butter if pan isn't non-stick). Mix in lemon juice and prawns and cook on low for 5 more minutes. Serve immediately.

Good Friday's Fish with Mango and Kiwifruit

Serves 2

- *4 fresh white fish fillets*
- *1 tbs. butter*
- *2 kiwifruit*
- *1 mango*

Brush fish with melted butter and on a hot grill or barbecue, grill each side for 3 - 5 minutes, depending on thickness. Peel and slice the kiwifruit and mango and sauté lightly in the remaining butter. Serve layered on top of fish.

Grilled Fish with Tomato Chutney Dressing

Serves 4

- *4 fresh white fish fillets*
- *2 tbs. drained capers*
- *Tomato chutney dressing (see Sauces)*

Grill fish until golden brown. Top with tomato chutney dressing and sprinkle with capers.

Optional: Delicious served with sautéed lemon potatoes and salad.

Herbed Barramundi

Serves 2

- *2 fresh barramundi fillets*
- *2 tbs. chopped flat-leaf parsley*
- *2 tbs. chopped basil leaves*
- *2 tbs. fresh lemon juice*

Char-grill barramundi for 3 minutes each side. Top with herbs and lemon juice and serve with roast vegetables ... Yummy!!

Lemon Grilled Fish

Serves 4

- *4 fresh white fish fillets*
- *1 - 2 tbs. lemon pepper seasoning*
- *1 whole spring onion, finely chopped*

Sprinkle fish generously with lemon pepper seasoning. Cover and refrigerate for 15 minutes. Cook fish under a preheated grill or BBQ until flesh is white and flakes easily when tested with a fork. Garnish with onion.

Moroccan Salmon

Serves 2. This is divine, everyone that we have served this to has requested the recipe!!

- *2 salmon steaks*
- *1 tbs. extra virgin olive oil*
- *Moroccan seasoning*

Place salmon on a non-stick baking tray. Coat each fillet thoroughly first with oil, then with seasoning. Bake at 160C for 15 minutes or to your liking.

Pan Fried Fish

Serves 4

- *4 fresh white fish fillets*
- *3 - 4 slices of stale bread, finely grated*
- *1 egg, beaten*
- *3 tbs. extra virgin olive oil*

Season bread generously with sea salt and pepper. Dip fillets into egg and then into breadcrumbs. Heat a heavy based frying pan, doused with olive oil. Cook the fish on both sides for 3 minutes, or until cooked to your liking, remove from heat and allow to rest.

Optional: Serve with tartare sauce and a lemon wedge.

Salmon & Spinach Filo

Serves 2

- *2 salmon steaks (without the skin)*
- *250g frozen spinach, thawed, excess liquid squeezed out*
- *4 sheets filo pastry*
- *Extra virgin olive oil spray*

Preheat oven 180C. Place spinach in a bowl and season with sea salt and pepper. Place 2 sheets of filo separately on a flat surface and spray with oil, lay remaining two on top. Place salmon in centre of each and top with spinach. Lightly spray with oil and fold pastry to enclose salmon. Again, lightly spray with oil and place on a non-stick baking tray. Bake for 25 minutes or until golden and cooked.

Optional: Crush a clove of garlic into the spinach for an enriching flavour. This is nice served with Horseradish cream.

Tony's Delicious Quick Mango Fish

Serves 4. Recipe from Tony Van Dijk.

- *4 pieces of fresh swordfish fillets*
- *4 tbs. extra virgin olive oil*
- *2 fresh mangoes*
- *Cracked pepper*

Coat fish liberally with extra virgin olive oil and cracked pepper. Cook on a medium heated BBQ surface or flat fry pan. Cook fish till you can see the flesh turning white up to half way through, and then grind some more cracked pepper onto the exposed non-cooked surface before flipping over. Serve with BBQ or pan-cooked fresh mango flesh.

Optional: Can substitute tinned mangoes if fresh are out of season.

Tuna Curry

Makes 2

- *400g tin tuna chunks*
- *1 onion, cut*
- *400g tin cream of mushroom soup*
- *2 tsp. curry powder*

Fry onion in a little water until soft. Add curry powder and stir.
Add soup mix and tuna and stir thoroughly and simmer for
5 minutes. Serve warm over rice.

Lamb

Laughter is brightest where food is best

Irish Proverb

Asian Style Lamb Cutlets

Serves 4

- 10 lamb cutlets
- ⅓ cup (80ml) dry sherry
- ⅓ cup (80ml) soy sauce

Trim fat from cutlets. Marinate cutlets in sherry and soy sauce for 10 minutes. Drain and reserve marinade. Heat grill on high. Grill cutlets each side, brushing occasionally with marinade.

Balti Curried Lamb

Makes 4. Our gorgeous friend Wendy Beattie's favourite!!

- 1 tbs. sunflower oil
- 1 green pepper, deseeded and cut into strips
- 500g lamb stir-fry
- 420g jar Balti curry sauce

Heat the oil and stir-fry the green pepper, remove from the pan and stir-fry the lamb until sealed on all sides. Pour in the jar of curry sauce and cook gently for 15 - 20 minutes. Five minutes before the end of cooking time add the green peppers.

Creamy Cashew Lamb Masala

Serves 4

- 400g lamb stir-fry
- 350g jar creamy cashew nut masala
- ½ cup (85g) sultanas
- ½ cup (80g) almonds, chopped

Place 3 tbs. water in a frying pan over medium heat. Add lamb and stir-fry until sealed on all sides. Pour in jar of masala and add sultanas. Gently cook for 15 minutes. In the last 5 minutes add the almonds.

Optional: Served over jasmine rice.

Lamb & Bacon Parcels

Serves 4

- 4 loin lamb chops
- 2 rashers of bacon, cut in half
- 4 tbs. wholegrain mustard
- 2 sheets puff pastry

Cut the meat from the bone and trim off fat. Cut the puff pastry sheets in half and spread each generously with mustard. Place the lamb in the middle of the pastry and top with a half-rasher of bacon. Seal edges and bake in 180C oven for 20 - 30 minutes or until golden brown.

Optional: For a presentable finish, baste the pastry with a beaten egg. Can substitute mustard with basil pesto for a change.

Lamb Pesto Cutlets

Serves 3. Everyone *loooooooooooooooves* these!

- *6 lamb cutlets*
- *3 tbs. basil pesto*
- *3 tbs. parmesan cheese*

Preheat oven to 180C. Place cutlets on a baking paper lined tray. Combine pesto and parmesan and dollop 1 tbs. of mixture on top of each cutlet. Place in the oven and cook for 20 - 30 minutes or until cooked through.

Note: Can also do on a BBQ, cook one side of the cutlets first before turning over and then place pesto and parmesan mixture on top of the cooked side.

Lamb Shank Casserole

Serves 4

- *4 lamb shanks*
- *1 large onion, coarsely chopped*
- *1 pkt French onion soup*
- *1 tsp. Worcestershire sauce*

Place lamb shanks and onions into a large saucepan. Mix soup and sauce together with about 3 cups of water and pour over shanks. Cook on low for 4 hours and serve over mashed potato.

Optional: This is a lovely casserole as is, but if you have some tomato sauce, add a couple of tbs. for colour and if you are like us and put vegetables in everything this is no exception. Add whatever veges are in your fridge, carrot, celery, broccoli, cauliflower, squash, Brussels sprouts etc.

Oat Crusted Lamb Cutlets

Serves 4

- *800g lamb cutlets*
- *1 cup (100g) small oats*
- *4 tbs. grated parmesan cheese*
- *2 eggs*

Preheat oven 190C. For best result put oats through food processor or blender, then combine them with parmesan cheese. Dip cutlets in beaten egg, then oat mixture to coat. Place on alfoil on a baking tray. Bake for 30 minutes or until golden brown.

Optional: Add 1 tbs. mixed herbs to the oats and parmesan for added flavour.

Roast Lamb

Makes 4 - 6. A recipe by the lovely Jan Neale. One we love to be invited to on a Sunday night.

- *1kg leg of lamb (or shoulder)*
- *1 sprig rosemary*
- *2 cloves garlic, sliced*
- *2 tbs. olive oil*

Cut a 2 cm slit across the lamb in several places and insert 6 rosemary leaves and a slice of garlic in each. Coat the baking dish with oil and bake in a 200C oven for about 1 hour. Serve with roast vegetables and gravy.

Rogan Josh

Makes 4

- *500g lamb neck fillet, cut into 2cm pieces*
- *1 onion, sliced*
- *1 yellow pepper, deseeded & sliced*
- *420g jar Rogan Josh sauce*

Place the lamb in a hot saucepan over a moderate heat with a smattering of water and cook until sealed on all sides, remove from the pan and keep warm. Add the onion until softened, then add the pepper, lamb and sauce, cook gently for 30 minutes. Serve with rice and pappadums.

Optional: Top with toasted almonds coarsely chopped.

Spring Lamb Rack with Dukkah Yoghurt

Serves 4

- *2 x 8 cutlet racks of lamb*
- *300g thick Greek yoghurt*
- *1 clove garlic, crushed*
- *2 tbs. dukkah, plus extra for garnishing*

Preheat oven to 200C. Place lamb in a baking dish and cook for 25 minutes for medium doneness. Combine yoghurt, garlic and dukkah in a small bowl and mix well. Serve 3 - 4 cutlets per person with yoghurt mix dolloped on top and a green salad. Garnish lamb with extra dukkah.

Tandoori Lamb

Makes 4. Another brilliant recipe from our treasured and talented chef 'Spud' Moore.

- *8 lamb cutlets*
- *2½ tbs. tandoori paste*
- *200g natural yoghurt*
- *Freshly chopped coriander*

Trim lamb cutlets of unwanted fat. Mix tandoori paste, half the yoghurt and half the coriander and coat lamb. Allow to stand in a covered bowl for 1 hour in the fridge. Pan-fry cutlets until ¾ cooked. Drizzle remaining yoghurt and tandoori over the top of the cooking cutlets and finally sprinkle with the remaining coriander...mmmmm!

Tangy Lamb Balls

Serves 4. A recipe from Perditta O'Connor ... *Try them!*

- *500g lamb mince*
- *1 tsp. curry powder*
- *3 tbs. sweet chilli sauce*
- *Juice of 1 lemon*

Place all ingredients into a large bowl and combine. Roll into patties and fry in a non-stick frying pan until crunchy on the outside (this means it is cooked well on the inside).

Optional: Add a clove of garlic to the mixture. Serve with jasmine rice and a mint yoghurt dipping sauce or roll into small balls and serve with sweet chilli sauce as a nibble on their own.

Pasta

Did you know: 'Al dente' is used to describe when pasta is cooked to perfection. 'Al dente' in Italian literally means "to the tooth". Pasta that is al dente should not be overly firm, nor should it be overly soft.

Good luck!!!

AB's Pasta

Serves 4. A recipe by Alistair Beattie that shocked me at its simplicity and taste!

- *350g pkt spaghetti*
- *4 rashers rindless bacon, diced*
- *1 cup (100g) pine nuts*
- *190g jar sun-dried tomato pesto*

While you are cooking pasta, fry bacon until brown. Toast pine nuts for 2 - 3 minutes in preheated 150C oven. When spaghetti is ready, drain and rinse with boiling water. Mix with 4 tbs. of pesto and toss through bacon and pine nuts. Add more pesto, if required.

Blue Broccoli Fusilli Pasta

Serves 4

- *500g pkt fusilli pasta*
- *1 large head broccoli, cut into florets*
- *125g blue cheese*
- *280g tub crème fraiche*

Add fusilli to a saucepan of boiling water. Cook for 8 minutes, then drain. Similarly, add broccoli to a saucepan of boiling water, boil for 5 minutes or until just cooked through. Drain. Meanwhile add blue cheese and crème fraiche to a frying pan over low heat and reduce to a thick, creamy sauce. Toss through broccoli and pasta, heat through and serve warm.

Optional: Serve topped with toasted pine nuts.

Florentine Carbonara

Serves 4. Recipe from Julie Stephens from Italy.
THIS IS TIMELESS!!

- *350g spaghetti*
- *5 rashes rindless bacon, diced*
- *2 eggs lightly beaten*
- *100g shaved parmesan cheese*

Bring a medium bowl of water to the boil. Add spaghetti and boil till al dente (around 8 minutes). While spaghetti is boiling, lightly fry bacon strips in a frying pan. Once spaghetti is cooked, drain (do not rinse) and add beaten eggs immediately, stirring through hot pasta. Add bacon, sprinkle with cheese and serve.

Optional: Fry bacon with a little garlic. Serve with French bread smothered with garlic butter.

Garden Penne Pasta

Serves 4

- *4 cups (300g) penne pasta*
- *4 tbs. extra virgin olive oil*
- *6 stems fresh basil, torn*
- *5 tomatoes, diced*

Add pasta to a saucepan of boiling water, stir immediately and cook uncovered for 12 minutes or until al dente, stirring occasionally. Drain and add the remaining ingredients, lightly toss to combine.

Optional: Fresh cracked pepper to taste.

Homemade Pasta

Serves 2. Rach's brother Spud taught her how to make this and it's the BEST homemade pasta you will taste - BRILLIANT!!

- *1 cup of OO Flour (or similar fine Italian flour)*
- *1 whole egg and also 1 egg yolk*
- *1 teaspoon of mixed herbs*

Mix all ingredients together till well combined (this takes a while so it may be best to use an electric mixer). Rest dough in a bowl in the fridge for 30 minutes. Sprinkle flour onto a bench and break the dough into 3 equal parts and roll out into rough rectanglular shaped strips (about 30 - 40 cms in length and about 10 - 15cms in width), roll until dough is about 2mm even in thickness. Starting from one length, roll and slice into 1cm (for fettuccine) or 2cm (for tagliatelle) strips. Sprinkle with flour to ensure the dough doesn't stick. Boil water in a medium sized saucepan and add pasta cooking for just 3 minutes. Drain water, and serve.

Optional: A beautiful serving suggestion Spud has was to heat some extra virgin olive oil in a non-stick frypan, add some sundried tomatoes, 1 tsp of crushed garlic. After lightly frying, add to pasta and sprinkle some parmesan cheese throughout. It was DIVINE!!!

Meg's Pasta

Serves 2. A recipe by Meg Wilson.

- *200g pasta of choice*
- *100g prosciutto, shredded*
- *1 ripe avocado, cubed*
- *3tbs. chilli oil*

Bring water to the boil. Add pasta and cook until tender. Remove and drain, add remaining ingredients and serve.

Optional: Prosciutto can be replaced by 100g cooked prawns.

Pasta with Crab & Lemon Cream Sauce

Serves 4. A recipe from the gorgeous Kirsty Morrison.

- *500g spiral pasta*
- *300ml cream*
- *1 lemon*
- *400g freshly cooked crab meat or 2 x 170g tin crab meat, drained*

Bring water to the boil. Add pasta and cook until tender. Meanwhile, finely grate the lemon rind then heat cream and rind in a medium sized saucepan; bring to boil. Add crabmeat and stir gently until heated through. Remove from heat and pour over pasta ... Yummmmmmmmmmmmmmm!!

Optional: This is really nice with ¼ cup of freshly chopped flat leaf parsley mixed through it.

Tagliatelle Alfredo

Serves 4

- *400g of tagliatelle (fresh fettuccine would be great)*
- *250ml cream*
- *120g good quality parmesan, grated*
- *1tbs. butter*

Pop the pasta inside boiling salted water, then take a pan and put the butter, cream and parmesan together. Simmer until it gets hot, but not boiling. When the pasta is done, drain it with a colander and add to the warm cream and mix ... Yummo!

Tip: Add a thread of oil to the water, it helps prevent fresh pasta sticking to one with another.

Veal Tortellini Soup

Serves 4. Recipe from Yolanda Lukowski.

- *1ltr. beef stock*
- *700ml tomato passata*
- *½ tsp. sugar*
- *375g veal tortellini*

Place the stock, passata and sugar in a large saucepan over medium heat and bring to a high simmer. Add the tortellini and cook for 8 minutes or until al dente. To serve, distribute tortellini evenly into serving bowls and pour over the soup.

Pork

The difference between 'involvement' and 'commitment'
is like a bacon and eggs breakfast;
the chicken was 'involved' - the pig was 'committed'.

Anonymous

Apricot & Mustard Pork Chops

Serves 4. Kim's father-in-law loves these!!

- *4 tbs. apricot jam*
- *2 tbs. Dijon mustard*
- *4 pork loin chops*
- *3 spring onions, finely chopped*
-

In a small saucepan over low heat, cook and stir apricot jam and mustard until jam melts, set aside. Place pork chops under grill and grill for 3 minutes each side. Brush with half the glaze and grill for another 3 minutes each side. Brush with the remaining glaze and grill a further 2 minutes or until juices run clear. Top with spring onions.

Optional: Serve over rice or with a lovely fresh salad.

Fried Sausages

Serves 4

- *8 sausages*
- *2 tbs. plain flour*
- *2 tbs. extra virgin olive oil*

Prick sausages with a fork, season flour with sea salt and pepper. Roll sausages in seasoned flour then gently fry in hot oil turning every 5 minutes for about 15 - 20 minutes or until browned.

Optional: Serve with gravy and mashed potatoes.

Ham on the Bone

Serves 8. Another by Kendra Horwood. *A Christmas Champion!*

- *½ ham on the bone*
- *150g ham glaze or a jar of marmalade*
- *30 cloves*
- *24 fresh, plump cherries*

Preheat oven 170C. Remove outer skin of ham and reserve (use when storing ham to keep moist). Using a sharp knife, score the fat into diamond shapes and stud the creases with cloves. Place ham on rack in a roasting tray and brush with glaze. Pour 1¼ cups of water into roasting pan. Bake ham for 25 minutes until golden, remove from oven and set aside. If there is liquid in the base of the pan, place on the stove and reduce over medium heat until syrupy then pour over ham before serving. Garnish with cherries before serving.

Pork 'Sticky' Stir-fry

Serves 4

- *500g pork stir-fry*
- *¼ cup (60ml) hoisin sauce*
- *¼ cup (60ml) soy sauce*
- *¼ cup (80g) honey*

Heat a non-stick frypan over medium to high heat. Add sauces and honey, allow to boil for 2 - 3 minutes until mixture thickens. Add the pork and cook, stirring, for 5 minutes or until cooked through ... Sticky but yummy!

Optional: Serve with fried rice and some green vegetables!

Pork & Bacon Wraps

Serves 4. D.E.L.I.C.I.O.U.S!

- *2 pork fillets*
- *4 tbs. basil pesto*
- *4 rashers bacon, rindless*
- *½ cup (120g) apple sauce*

Cut pork fillets in half. Spread outside with ⅔ of basil pesto. Wrap bacon around fillets to cover outside. Bake in 180C oven for 25 - 30 minutes or until pork is cooked. Mix remaining pesto with apple sauce and heat until almost boiling, serve with fillets.

Pork & Coconut Satay Sticks

Serves 4. Yummy!

- *200ml coconut milk*
- *2 tbs. crunchy peanut butter*
- *2 tsp. curry powder*
- *500g pork stir-fry*

Mix the first 3 ingredients together and season with sea salt and pepper until blended. Add the pork and marinate overnight. Soak bamboo sticks in water before threading with pork. Cook on a hot grill for 10 – 15 minutes turning constantly so as not to burn. Continue to glaze throughout.

Tip: Place a sheet of non stick baking paper on the grill, pierce some holes to allow juices to run away. This will prevent the kebabs sticking to the cooking surface.

Optional: Serve with a lovely fresh Mediterranean salad.
Can substitute pork for chicken.

Pork Spare Ribs

Serves 4. Kim's Mum does these SOOOO effortlessly and they are SOOOO nice!!

- *8 pork spare ribs*
- *375g bottle honey, soy and garlic marinade*
  (if you can't buy this see Sauces for marinade recipe)

Boil ribs first for 5 - 10 minutes to rid excess fat. Drain and place ribs on a large non-stick baking tray. Cover both sides of each rib generously with marinade. Pop in the refrigerator for at least half an hour before cooking. Place under grill, cooking 5 minutes each side until juices run clear. Continue basting throughout.

Optional: Serve with rice and topped with crunchy snow peas.

Pork Tenderloin Bake

Serves 6

- *600g pork tenderloin*
- *400g can tomato soup*
- *1 pkt French onion soup*
- *2 tbs. Worcestershire sauce*

Place tenderloin in a casserole dish that has a lid. Combine remaining ingredients, mix and pour over meat. Place lid on the dish and bake in 150C oven for 1 hour. Cut meat into 1 inch slices and use the soup as a flavoursome gravy.

Pork Tenderloin with Mustard Sauce

Serves 6. This is a great dinner party main.

- *600g pork tenderloin*
- *¼ cup (60ml) soy sauce*
- *¼ cup (60ml) bourbon*
- *2 tbs. brown sugar*

Mix soy sauce, bourbon and sugar. Marinate pork in the mixture for 2 - 3 hours, basting occasionally. Remove pork and bake in a preheated 150C oven for 1 hour, basting occasionally. Remove and slice.

Optional: This is sensational served with the mustard sauce (see Sauces).

Rich Tomato Pork

Serves 4. A recipe from Tanya Ormsby

- *4 pork chops*
- *2 cloves garlic, crushed*
- *400g tin of seasoned diced tomatoes,*
  e.g. basil and garlic, or oregano and basil
- *½ cup (125ml) cream*

In a non-stick pan fry pork until golden on both sides, add garlic
and tinned tomatoes, bring to boil then let simmer for 2½ hrs
(you may need a little more tomato mixture, depending on size of
fillets).   Half an hour before serving, add cream and turn up the
heat to thicken.

Optional: Serve with mashed potatoes and beans with pine nuts.

Roast Pork

Serves 8. Recipe by Lisa Darr.

- *1 kg roast leg of pork*
- *3 tbs. extra virgin olive oil*

Preheat oven 220C. Rub 1 tbs. oil onto rind of pork. Grind sea salt
over rind and rub into pork. Pour remaining oil into baking dish and
place in 220C oven for 20 minutes. Reduce heat to 180C and cook
for 1 hour (or half hour per 500g).

*Optional: Serve with roast vegetables, best gravy ever and apple
sauce. Kim's husband, Glen scores the skin and bathes it with fresh
lemon juice and loads of ground sea salt making a divine crackling!*

Sausage Bake

Serves 4. So easy, so tasty, so cheap!

- *6 thick sausages*
- *500g chopped vegetables*
  (celery, onion, carrot, broccoli, cauliflower, etc).
- *100g cheddar cheese, grated*
- *400g tin cream of mushroom soup*

Combine all in a casserole dish and season with sea salt and pepper. Bake covered for 45 minutes at 150C, uncover, stir and bake a further 15 minutes.

Tangy Pork Chops

Serves 4

- *4 pork chops*
- *4 tbs. honey*
- *2 tbs.Worcestershire sauce*
- *4 tbs. tomato sauce*

Lightly brown pork chops under grill. Place in a shallow baking dish. Combine remaining ingredients and pour over chops. Cover and bake at 170C for 45 minutes.

Vegetarian Mains

Girls are like phones ... We love to be held and talked to but if you press the wrong button you'll be disconnected!

Anonymous

Aubergine & Sweet Potato Curry

Serves 4. This is really yummy!

- *2 onions, peeled and sliced*
- *1 aubergine, chopped into 2cm pieces*
- *1 medium to large size sweet potato, peeled and chopped into large chunks*
- *350g Korma mildly spiced organic sauce*

Simmer onion in water until tender. Remove from pan and set aside. In a non-stick fry pan, fry aubergines until browned evenly. Return onions to pan with sweet potato and Korma sauce. Fill half the empty jar with water and add to pan. Simmer for 20 - 30 minutes until the potato and aubergine are tender.

Optional: Serve with rice and pappadums.

Baked Ravioli

Serves 4 - 6

- *500g ravioli*
- *500g of organic pasta sauce*
- *100g parmesan cheese, grated (reserve some for topping)*
- *2 sprigs parsley, chopped*

Preheat oven to 190C. Cook ravioli in boiling water until it is just cooked, drain. Line a casserole dish with a thin layer of pasta sauce, add a layer of ravioli and sprinkle a layer of cheese and a touch of parsley. Repeat layering process finishing with a layer of ravioli, topped with remaining pasta sauce and cheese. Bake for 15 minutes or until cheese is melted and bubbly. Cut into squares as you would lasagne.

Optional: Serve hot with salad, homemade potato chips or just by itself.

Cheesy, Cabbage Pasta Bake

Serves 4

- *2 cups (250g) penne pasta, cooked*
- *1 Savoy cabbage, shredded*
- *125g grated cheddar cheese*
- *2 slices of buttered bread, finely grated*

Preheat the oven to 220C. In a baking dish, place alternating layers of pasta, cabbage and cheese and season between layers. Sprinkle with breadcrumbs and cheese and bake in a 180C oven for 10 - 15 minutes or until bubbling.

Coconut Rice

Serves 4

- 330g basmati rice
- 2 x 400ml cans coconut milk
- ½ cup (110g) sultanas
- Good pinch of turmeric

In a large saucepan over high heat, combine rice, coconut milk and 2 cups of water and bring to the boil. Reduce heat, add sultanas, cover and simmer on low heat for 25 minutes or until liquid is absorbed and rice is tender. Stir often. Add turmeric for colour.

Green Coconut Curry

Serves 4 and is really, really tasty!

- 4 tbs. green curry paste
- 400ml can coconut milk
- 250g pkt sweet potato
- 400g mixed vegetables
  (broccoli, carrots, zucchinis, green beans, etc)

Heat a wok or a deep frying pan (with a lid) to low heat. Add the green curry paste and gently stir-fry for a minute or so. Add the sweet potato and coconut milk with 1 cup water. Cover with a lid, and bring to the boil and gently simmer until the sweet potato is almost cooked. Add your mixed vegetables (exclude soft veges, like zucchini and squash, etc.) and continue to simmer for another 10 minutes. When the sweet potato is starting to fall apart, add soft vegetables. Simmer for another 5 minutes. When all vegetables are cooked and the sweet potato has broken down to almost a puree, the dish is ready.

Optional: This is delicious served over rice.

Green Bean Curry

Serves 4. This is easy and delicious!

- *500g fine green beans*
- *2 tbs. red curry paste*
- *1 red pepper or a can of bamboo shoots or any other veges you have in the fridge*
- *1½ ltr. vegetable stock*

Top and tail the beans and cut in half or thirds, if really long. In a saucepan heat the curry paste stirring continuously for approx. 1 minute. Add stock and beans and bring to a rapid boil. Cook for 15 - 20 minutes, halfway through, add red pepper. Continue to cook until the beans are well done and have absorbed the flavour of the curry-chicken broth.

Optional: Serve over rice.

Mixed Bean Korma

Serves 4

- *420g can mixed beans, drained*
- *125g fine green beans, cooked*
- *500g jar creamy korma curry sauce*
- *½ tub natural yoghurt*

Place the mixed beans, green beans and korma sauce in a saucepan and simmer gently. Simmer for 10 - 15 minutes. Dollop with yoghurt and serve.

Mushroom Risotto

Serves 4

- 250g mushrooms, sliced
- 200g arborio rice
- 1 ltr. vegetable stock
- 125g shaved parmesan cheese

Lightly fry mushrooms in a non-stick pan. Add rice and stir until combined. Pour stock in another pan and boil. Stir ⅔ cup stock into the rice. Stir until all absorbed. Continue adding stock in small quantities, stirring regularly, until gone. When this process is finished, add cheese and season.

Optional: Add a chopped onion with mushrooms if desired.

Original Risotto

Serves 4

- 2 tbs. olive oil
- 1½ tbs. butter
- 200g arborio rice
- 1 ltr. vegetable stock

Simmer the stock on the stove. In a separate, heavy-based saucepan, heat the oil and butter. Add the rice and stir to coat with the oil and butter. Stir for 2 minutes until you hear a cracking sound and the rice becomes translucent. Add ½ cup of the stock and stir until it is absorbed. Continue adding more liquid in this manner until the rice is cooked. Taste after 15 - 20 minutes. The rice should be firm to bite. Remove from heat and add whatever flavourings you want. Season and stir.

Parsnip Pie

Serves 4.   *You'll be surprised!*

- *1 sheet puffed pastry*
- *3 eggs*
- *250g ricotta cheese*
- *2 x 250g pkt roast parsnips*

Bake parsnips to manufacturer's instructions. Meanwhile, line a quiche dish with baking paper onto which lay the sheet of puffed pastry. Beat eggs well then add ricotta. Season with sea salt and pepper and continue beating until smooth. Once parsnips are done, cut in half and spread over the base of the pastry, pour in filling. Bake in a preheated 180C oven for 30 minutes.

Pasta with Tomato & Basil

Serves 4. The kids will love this, too.

- *4 cups (300g) of pasta*
- *400ml passata*
- *½ bunch freshly torn basil leaves*
- *100g parmesan cheese, shaved*

Cook pasta on high for 8 minutes and drain. Add it to the simmering sugo and most of the parmesan. When the pasta is al dente, stir though the basil leaves and serve sprinkled with remaining parmesan and a basil leaf to garnish.

Sour Cream Quiche

Serves 4 – 6 ... This is s.e.n.s.a.t.i.o.n.a.l!

- *1 sheet puffed pastry*
- *3 eggs*
- *320g sour cream*
- *Filling; choose from feta, tinned corn, asparagus, baby spinach, semi-dried tomatoes, onion, tuna, chicken, bacon, pineapple ... Whatever you like!*

Line a non-stick quiche dish with puffed pastry. Beat eggs and sour cream. Pour over chosen filling. To taste, add sea salt and pepper and bake in 180C oven for 30 minutes or until set.

Optional: Kim's Mum, Jennette, often adds a splash of tomato and Worcestershire sauces or curry powder to the egg mix for extra flavour.

Vegetable Lasagne

Serves 6. Thanks to Kimmy Morrison for this terrific and very easy dinner!

- *6 sheets lasagna pasta*
- *200g cheddar cheese, grated*
- *1 sweet potato*
- *500g jar vegetable pasta sauce*

Preheat oven to 150C. Peel and slice sweet potato then boil till soft, drain liquid and mash. Line a baking tray with baking paper. Place 2 sheets of lasagna side by side. Lightly cover with layer of cheese. Spoon over some mashed potato - covering cheese. Pour over pasta sauce to cover mash potato. Repeat layering process till last lasagna sheet has been used and cheese, potato and sauce has been laid over the top of the last sheet. Finish off with ½ cup of cheese. Bake for 35 minutes, or until cheese is slightly golden.

Optional: Fabulous with salad, chips or even more vegetables.

4 Ingredients

Desserts

Kindness is like sugar, it makes life taste a little sweeter

Carla Yerovi

Apple Crumble

Serves 4 - 6. A golden oldie … This is really easy and really tasty!

- *395g tinned apples*
- *½ cup (115g) soft butter*
- *¾ cup (165g) brown sugar*
- *1 cup (175g) plain flour*

Quarter and core the apples. Slice the quarters into 1.5cm-wide wedges. Place the apple wedges in the greased dish. Sprinkle with 2 tbs. brown sugar. Mix remaining ingredients in a bowl with a knife until crumbly. Spread over apple and bake in a preheated 200C oven for 30 minutes or until the crumble topping is golden and the apples are tender when tested with a skewer but still hold their shape. Serve warm with the cream or ice-cream.

Optional: Sprinkle the apple with ½ tsp. mixed spice before spreading with the crumble.

Chestnut & Brandy Meringues

Makes 4

- *100g tin sweetened chestnut puree*
- *100g cooked chestnuts, crumbled*
- *300ml cream with brandy*
- *6 meringue nests*

Mix the chestnut purée and pieces together. Stir in the brandy. Roughly fold in the créme fraîche creating a marble effect. Place a meringue on each plate and dollop a large spoonful of the chestnut mix on top.

Optional: Top with shaved chocolate if desired.

Barbie Bananas

Serves 4. A recipe from Tanya Ormsby.

- *4 bananas*
- *125ml Baileys Irish cream*
- *4 scoops ice-cream*

Put the whole bananas on the BBQ - skins and all! Leave for 4 - 5 minutes, slit the top and add enough Baileys to prevent overflowing. Leave for a further 1 - 2 minutes, remove and serve with ice-cream.

Basic Cheesecake

Serves

- *250g cream cheese, softened*
- *400g condensed milk*
- *1 sachet gelatine*
- *Bickie base (as follows)*

In medium bowl, beat cream cheese until smooth. Add condensed milk and mix until combined. Dissolve gelatine in 3 tbs. of boiling water, stirring vigorously until dissolved then add to mixture. Pour into above bickie base and chill for at least 1 hour prior to serving.

Optional: Delicious covered with fresh strawberries and kiwi fruit.

Bickie Base

- *200g sweet digestive bickies*
- *6 tbs. butter, melted*

Blend the bickies in a blender or food processor. Transfer to a bowl and add the melted butter. Mix well and then press into the bottom of a cheesecake dish. Chill before using.

Optional: Add a dash of nutmeg or cinnamon for flavour.

Blue Chockie Mousse

Serves 4. This is berry, berry nice!

- *2 punnet blueberries*
- *200g dark chocolate*
- *300ml thickened cream*

Evenly place blueberries into the bottom of four small ramekins. Melt chocolate carefully in a bowl in the microwave, stir every 15 seconds. Remove and allow to cool. Beat cream until soft peaks form, then fold in the melted chocolate. Spoon the mixture over the blueberries and serve immediately.

Blueberry Puffs

Makes 4

- *2 sheets puff pastry*
- *2 punnet blueberries*
- *1 cup (200g) caster sugar*
- *2 tbs. butter, melted*

Preheat oven to 180C. Cut pastry in ½, allowing for 4 pieces. Thoroughly combine blueberries and ¾ of the sugar, and then place in the center of the pastry, roll up and brush with butter. Make a few fine cuts on the top and sprinkle with remaining sugar. Place on a lined baking tray and bake for 15 - 20 minutes, or until golden brown.

Optional: Serve warm with a scoop of creamy, vanilla ice-cream.

Chocolate Mousse

Serves 4. This is a dreamy Chocolate Mousse.

- *100g dark chocolate*
- *1 tbs. butter*
- *2 eggs*
- *½ cup (125ml) thickened cream*

Melt chocolate with butter carefully in a bowl in the microwave, stir every 15 seconds until smooth. Remove and cool for a few minutes, then stir in 2 beaten egg yolks and half a cup lightly whipped cream. Whip 2 eggwhites until soft peaks form, then gently fold into chocolate mixture. Spoon into small dishes or glasses and refrigerate for 3 hours, or until firm.

Optional: Drizzle 1 tsp. of Grand Marnier, cognac or rum over each mousse. Serve with extra whipped cream and fresh raspberries and strawberries, dusted with icing sugar.

Chrissie's Caramel Tart

Serves 6. Recipe from Rach's great grandmother Chrissie Moore.

- *1 sheet sweet short pastry*
- *400g tin condensed milk*
- *1 cup (250ml) cream, whipped*
- *1 tsp. butter*

Place unopened tin of condensed milk into a large saucepan generously covering tin with water, boil for 2 hours to turn the milk into caramel, (check every 30 minutes to ensure tin is covered in water, top up when necessary so the tin doesn't burst). Preheat oven to 180C. Grease pie dish with butter and line with sheet of pastry. Place in oven for 10 minutes, or until golden brown. Pour cooled caramel into pastry shell. Spoon over thickened whipped cream generously ... *As easy as 1,2,3*!

Creamy Cognac Ice-cream

Serves 4 - 6. A recipe by Lisa Darr. This is sooooooooooooooooooooo yummy!!!

- *500g crème fraiche*
- *1½ cups (187g) golden icing sugar*
- *4 tbs. cognac*

Sift icing sugar into a large bowl. Add crème fraiche and cognac and whisk well, continuing to whisk until the mixture thickens slightly. Pour the mix into a baking paper lined loaf tin, cover with cling wrap and freeze overnight ... A great Christmas pudding accompaniment.

Creme Brulee

Serves 4. If you are in the bad books and want to work your way into the good books ... THIS WILL DO IT!!!

- *400ml cream*
- *1 vanilla bean, split and scraped*
- *5 egg yolks*
- *½ cup (110g) brown sugar*

Combine cream and vanilla bean in a medium saucepan and bring just to boil. Leave to infuse for 15 minutes. Meanwhile, lightly beat egg yolks and half the sugar until well combined. Strain infused cream over yolk mixture and whisk briefly to blend. Return cream and egg mixture to same cleaned saucepan and stir over very low heat until custard thickens enough to coat the back of a spoon. Pour into 4 ramekins and refrigerate (covered) for about 4 hours. Just before serving, remove from fridge and place in a baking tray full of cold water and ice. Cover surface of each brulee generously with remaining sugar. Place under grill until sugar melts, making a shiny crust, or use a blow torch to brown if you have one.

Tip: The top should be hard, and when cracked with the spoon, will give a wonderful contrast to the creamy bottom.

Cookie & Cream Truffles

Makes 40. This recipe *R.O.C.K.S!*

- *500g Oreo cookies*
- *250g cream cheese, softened*
- *400g milk chocolate*
- *100g white chocolate*

In a blender, crush cookies. Pour into a bowl, add cream cheese and mix until there are no traces of white. Using a teaspoon, roll mixture into balls, place on a baking paper lined tray and refrigerate for 45 minutes. Break milk chocolate into pieces and place in a microwaveable container, melt gradually checking and stirring every 20 seconds until smooth. Coat balls thoroughly with melted chocolate, place back into fridge to cool. Finally melt remaining white chocolate and using a fork drizzle over milk chocolate balls.

Lemon Syllabub

Serves 4

- *300g tub whipping cream*
- *50g caster sugar*
- *50ml white wine*
- *Zest and juice from ½ lemon*

Whip the cream and sugar together until soft peaks form. Stir in the wine, most of the lemon zest and the juice. Spoon into glasses or bowls, sprinkle with the remaining zest.

Optional: Serve with almond thins or fresh berries.

Frozen Fruit Yoghurt Soft Serve

Serves 4 - 6. A sensational recipe from Cyndi O'Meara.

- *2 cups fresh fruit, (bananas, strawberries, mango, blueberries, etc) all roughly chopped*
- *½ cup (160g) manuka honey*
- *450g organic natural yoghurt*

Process fruit in a blender until smooth. Add honey and yoghurt and mix thoroughly. Pour into a covered container and freeze. Remove from freezer 20 - 30 minutes before serving.

Fruit Sundae Snacks

Makes 6

- *12 strawberries, washed, hulled and chopped*
- *3 cups of fruit chopped (such as cherries, apples, bananas, seedless grapes, kiwifruit, peaches)*
- *6 waffle cones*
- *1 tbs. shredded coconut*

Blend the strawberries till smooth, and set aside. Place the fruit in a bowl and toss to combine. Spoon fruit evenly among the cones. Drizzle with strawberry puree, top with coconut and serve.

Grilled Mango Halves with Lime

Serves 4

- *3 large mangoes*
- *1 lime*
- *2 tbs. brown sugar*

Cut each mango in half, cutting around the seed and leaving the skin on. Score the skin of each half with a sharp knife making an X pattern. Squeeze lime juice onto the mango halves. Sprinkle the fruit with the brown sugar. Place the mangoes on a preheated and oiled BBQ plate and cook, sugared side down, for 2 - 3 minutes.

Optional: Serve with a sorbet. A great BBQ dessert.

Ice-Cream with a Twist

Serves 2

- *2 bowls vanilla ice-cream*
- *1 punnet strawberries, washed and hulled*
- *2 tbs. caramelised balsamic vinegar*

Place vanilla ice-cream in a bowl. Slice strawberries and mix with caramelised balsamic vinegar. Once combined, tip over ice-cream and serve.

Key Lime Pie

Serves 8. This is DELECTABLE!!

- *4 large egg yolks*
- *400g can of condensed milk*
- *4 limes, juiced*
- *Readymade sweet pie base*

Use an electric mixer and beat the egg yolks until they are thick and turn to a light yellow – don't over mix. Turn the mixer off and add the condensed milk. Turn speed to low and mix in half the lime juice. Once the juice is incorporated, add the other half and the zest of one lime, continue to mix until blended (just a few seconds). Pour the mixture into the pie base and bake for 12 minutes at 150C to set.

Optional: Serve with whipped cream.

Microwave Fondue

Serves 2. Always looking for quick and tasty desserts, we devised this fantastic little treat.

- *200g dark chocolate*
- *½ cup (125ml) cream*
- *2 tbs. orange zest*

Warm cream and orange zest in a saucepan, slowly. Break chocolate and melt in microwave, checking every 20 seconds. When melted add to warm cream. Stir well and when warm pour into a bowl.

Optional: Serve with a plate of freshly sliced fruit and marshmallows for dipping.

Pavlova

Serves 6 - 8

- *2 tsp. cornflour*
- *1 cup (200g) caster sugar*
- *1 tsp. vanilla*
- *4 eggwhites*

Preheat the oven to 180C. Line a baking tray with baking paper. Beat the eggwhites until soft peaks form and gradually beat in the sugar. Beat until the mixture is thick and the sugar is dissolved. Carefully fold in the cornflour and vanilla essence. Spoon onto the baking paper on the tray. Reduce the oven heat to 150C and place in oven, bake for 1 hour.

Tip: For best result, eggs should be at room temperature.

Optional: Allow to cool completely before decorating with the whipped cream and sliced fruit. Karen Fitzgerald advised that "If you don't have cornflour, use vinegar!"

Poached Pears

Serves 6. A recipe from Wendy Beattie. Simply a sweet success!

- *6 firm ripe, pears*
- *½ cup (125ml) white wine*
- *Easy mocha sauce (see Sauces)*

Peel skin from pears and place upright in a microwaveable bowl. Pour wine and ⅓ cup water over the pears, return lid and cook on high for 10 minutes, or until soft. Remove and allow to cool in wine. Once cold, remove pears from wine and place in serving bowl, lavish with mocha sauce and serve.

Praline Fondue

Serves 4 - 6

- ½ cup (100g) caster sugar
- 200g toasted almonds
- 500ml cream
- 2 tbs. cornflour

Put caster sugar into a small saucepan, place over a low heat and leave until sugar is golden brown. Add almonds. Pour onto a lightly greased cake tin and allow to cool completely. Grind finely. Place cream into fondue pot, blend in cornflour and stir until thickened. Stir in praline. Serve with fresh fruit, marshmallows, etc.

Optional: Add a dash of vanilla essence.

Roasted Honey Pears with Honey Cream

Serves 4. Your *mummy-in-law* will love it, and you!!!!

- 3 firm, ripe pears
- 4 tbs. honey
- 2 tbs. brown sugar
- 300ml cream, whipped

Cut pears into quarters and remove cores. Place in an ovenproof dish, drizzle with ¼ cup honey and sprinkle with brown sugar. Pour ½ cup water around pears. Bake uncovered at 180C for 30 minutes, or until just soft. Place 3 pear quarters on four serving plates. Drizzle pan juices over pears. Mix whipped cream and ¼ cup honey together until combined. Serve over pears.

Optional: Add ¼ tsp. cinnamon to cream and honey for a lovely flavour.

For The Children

Children are one third of our population and all of our future.

Select Panel for the Promotion of Child Health, 1981

Savoury

Bugs in Rugs

Makes 12

- *3 slices brown bread*
- *½ cup (250ml) tomato sauce*
- *¼ cup (55g) butter, melted*
- *12 cocktail frankfurters*

Preheat oven 180C. Pierce frankfurters all over with a fork. Spread tomato sauce on bread, then cut into quarters. Place a frankfurter diagonally on each quarter of bread. Bring up edges and secure with a toothpick. Brush liberally with the melted butter. Place on greased baking tray and bake for 10 minutes until bread is crisp and lightly brown. Serve warm.

Optional: Sprinkle with poppy seeds before baking.

Coronation Chicken Fingers

Makes 1

- *2 thick slices of bread*
- *100g jar Coronation chicken*
- *2 slices of cheese*
- *Shredded lettuce to serve*

Lay bread on a baking tray and pop under the grill, toast 1 side then flip. Spread untoasted side with chicken and top with cheese.
Pop back under grill until cheese begins to bubble. Remove, allow to cool, cut into thirds creating 'Fingers' and serve topped with shredded lettuce.

Egg in a Hole

Makes 1

- *¼ tbs. butter*
- *1 slice brown bread*
- *1 free-range egg*

Heat frying pan and melt butter, cut a hole in the bread to fit the egg. Place bread in frying pan and crack egg into hole. Cook on one side until it just firms, flip and cook, till desired doneness.

Fish Cocktails

Makes 24

- *250g fresh white fish fillets*
- *3 tbs. plain flour*
- *1 eggwhite*
- *½ cup (60g) cornflakes, chrushed*

Preheat oven 180C. Cut fish into 3 cm cubes. Coat in flour and shake off excess. Whisk eggwhite in small bowl. Dip fish, one piece at a time in eggwhite, coat with cornflake crumbs. Place in a single layer on an oven tray and bake for 15 minutes, or until golden.

Gourmet Baked Beans on Toast

Makes 4. These are great!

- *4 thick slices bread, crust removed*
- *420g can baked beans*
- *2 tsp. butter*
- *100g cheddar cheese, grated*

Preheat oven 220C. Butter both sides of bread slices and press into 4 holes of a muffin tray. Bake for 5 - 10 minutes or until the bread is crisp and golden. Heat the baked beans in a pan over low heat until just warm. Spoon the baked beans into the bread cup and sprinkle with the grated cheese.

Italian Chicken

Makes 4 - 6

- *2 chicken breasts*
- *2 tbs. extra virgin olive oil*
- *1 onion, chopped*
- *350g tomato and roasted pepper organic pasta sauce*

Tenderise breasts, slice and then brown in oil. Push to one side and sauté onions until tender. Stir in spaghetti sauce and cover pan. Simmer for 10 - 12 minutes or until chicken is tender, and serve with pasta.

Mini Hotdogs

Makes 8

- *1 sheet puff pastry*
- *1 egg*
- *8 cocktail frankfurters*
- *Tomato sauce to serve*

Cut thawed pastry into 8. Brush with beaten egg before placing a frankfurter across each pastry piece. Wrap opposite ends of pastry around the frankfurter. Brush with egg again. Bake in 180C for 10 - 15 minutes or until golden. Serve with a bowl of tomato sauce for dipping.

Mini Pizzas

Makes 2. Thanks, Michelle Fredericks.

- *2 English muffins sliced in half*
- *4 tsp. tomato paste*
- *3 rashers of bacon*
- *4 tbs. grated mozzarella cheese*

Slice English muffin in half, spread pizza paste; lightly fry bacon pieces and scatter on top of paste and top with cheese ...
Quick and easy!

Parmesan Twists

A great little recipe from Meredith Mullaly

- *1 sheet puff pastry*
- *4 tbs. grated parmesan cheese*

Smother the sheet of puff pastry with parmesan. Cut in half, and then cut into 2 cm wide strips. Twist and bake in a hot oven for approximately 5 minutes or until golden brown. Allow to cool and store in an airtight container. For an added flavour, you can sprinkle with paprika prior to baking.

Vegemite Twists

- *1 sheet puff pastry*
- *1 tbs. vegemite*

Exactly as above, except substitute parmesan with vegemite or marmite (no paprika).

Popcorn Chicken

Serves 4

- *4 chicken breasts*
- *1 - 2 tbs. cajun powder*
- *1½ cups of basmati rice*
- *½ cup of extra virgin olive oil*

Bring a medium saucepan with 3 cups of water to boil. Add rice and simmer till cooked, drain and set aside. Tenderise chicken lightly and cut into small pieces. Put into a frying pan with oil and stir over a medium heat. Before chicken has whitened, shake on cajun powder to taste. Leave cooking until well done and crispy black (looks burnt but tastes yummy). Serve with rice.

Porcupines

Serves 4. We learnt to cook these in Grade 8 Home Ec. class – they're great!!

- *½ kg mince*
- *½ cup (110g) cooked rice*
- *1 egg*
- *400g can condensed tomato soup*

Combine mince, egg and rice in a bowl and mix well. Season with sea salt and pepper. Roll mixture into small rissole like balls = 'Porcupines.' Place in casserole dish. Mix tomato soup with ¾ of same can of water and pour over porcupines. Cook in moderate oven for about 1 hour. Serve with mashed potato and vegetables.

Optional: Add an onion, finely chopped, to the mince for a yummy flavour.

Sandwich Rollups

- 4 slices brown bread
- 1 tbs. butter
- Sandwich fillings; ham, cheese, marmite, cheese, etc
- Bunch of fresh, long chives

Remove crusts. Lay slices of bread on a flat surface and with a rolling pin, roll out until bread is quite thin. Butter lightly and cover each slice with chosen fillings. Roll tightly and cut into thirds. Tie with a sprig of chives.

Savoury Dip

- 600ml sour cream
- 1 pkt chicken soup mix
- Food colourings
- Assortment of fresh vegetable sticks

Combine sour cream and soup mix. Separate mixture into three small bowls and tint with whatever food colourings you have. Serve with vege sticks.

Simple Spaghetti

Serves 2. A recipe by Heather and Alexis Wallis … Your kids will love it, too!

- *½ packet of penne pasta*
- *1 tbs. butter*
- *100g cheddar cheese, grated*
- *½ cup (125ml) tomato sauce*

Cook pasta, drain and place in saucepan. Add butter mixing until melted. Add tomato sauce and cheese and mix until cheese starts to melt. Serve hot.

Optional: Sprinkle with toasted pine nuts.

Spaghetti Bolognese

Serves 4

- *350g pkt spaghetti*
- *500g lean organic mince*
- *500g organic mushroom or vegetable pasta sauce*
- *100g parmesan cheese, shaved*

Put 2 tbs. of water in a frying pan and add mince, cook on medium heat till pink colouring has just disappeared. Add pasta sauce and stir, lower heat and cover for 6 minutes. Boil water and add spaghetti to boil, simmer for 6 minutes, or until al dente.
Drain pasta and place equal portions of pasta in 4 bowls.
Add mince and sprinkle with cheese to finish.

Sweet Chicken with Cornflakes

Serves 4 - 6. Recipe from Cyndi O'Meara. We *loooove* this!

* *750g organic chicken breast fillets*
* *200ml organic plain yoghurt*
* *2 handfuls cornflakes, ground*
* *100g parmesan cheese, grated*

Preheat oven to 180C. Combine cornflakes and cheese together in one bowl, and place yoghurt in another bowl. Coat chicken with yoghurt and then cornflake and cheese mixture. Bake in oven for 20 - 30 minutes, depending on size of chicken breasts.

Too Easy Chicken Nuggets

Serves 2. These are requested at least twice a week!

* *2 chicken breasts, cut into bite-size pieces*
* *1 cup (130g) breadcrumbs*
* *½ cup (130g) organic mayonnaise*
* *1 tbs. butter, melted*

Preheat oven to 180C. Coat chicken with mayonnaise and roll in breadcrumbs. Lay on a baking paper lined baking tray. Drizzle with a little butter and bake for 20 minutes.

Tuna With Spaghetti

Makes 2. A recipe from the lovely Alice Beattie!

- *400g tin spaghetti*
- *400g tin tuna chunks, drained*
- *½ cup (50g) cheddar cheese, grated*
- *½ cup (65g) breadcrumbs*

Combine tuna and spaghetti. Place in baking dish. Sprinkle with cheese and breadcrumbs and bake in moderate oven until golden brown.

Vegetable Shapes

Serves 2. These put a thrill into eating vegetables!

- *1 potato*
- *100g piece pumpkin*
- *Extra virgin olive oil spray*
- *Metal shapes eg., stars, hearts, animal shapes etc*

Slice potato and pumpkin into 2cm thick slices. Cut out as many shapes as possible. Spray with oil and bake in 180C oven 15 - 20 minutes turning halfway through.

Optional: Keep scraps and make a mashed potato and pumpkin on another night.

Sweet

The laughter of a child is the light of a house

Anonymous

Apple & Nutella Wraps

Makes 8. Yummy!

- *2 sheets puffed pasty*
- *8 tbs. Nutella*
- *400g tin of apples*
- *2 tbs. icing sugar*

Cut your puffed pastry sheets in quarters. Generously smear nutella diagonally from one end to the other. Place stewed apple along nutella. Fold opposite ends over mixture. Bake in preheated 180C oven for 15 - 20 minutes. Sprinkle with icing sugar for decoration.

Various Options:

- *Add sultanas*

- *Nutella and banana*

- *Stacks of fresh raspberries and served topped with a dollop of freshly whipped cream*

- *Honey, apples and cinnamon*

- *Raspberry jam and chunks of dark chocolate*

Apricot Dream Balls

Makes 24

- *¾ cup (115g) dried fruit medley*
- *¼ cup (40g) dried apricots*
- *2 tbs. coconut milk*
- *Plate of desiccated coconut*

Place fruit medley, apricots and coconut milk into a food processor or your hand-held mixer, and whiz until mixture comes together. Shape into balls and roll in coconut. Chill until firm.

Optional: We have used condensed milk and tahini instead of coconut milk and both were yummy.

Baked Custard

Serves 4. A recipe from our muchly loved 'Grandma' Jennette McCosker.

- *500ml milk*
- *2 eggs*
- *2 tbs. sugar*
- *½ tsp. vanilla essence*

Put milk and sugar in a saucepan and bring to the boil stirring occasionally. Add vanilla essence and remove from heat. Pour about ¼ cup of boiling milk into beaten eggs while stirring. This warms the eggs and prevents curdling. Pour the egg mixture into the remaining milk mixture. Stir briskly until well combined. Pour into a small baking dish and bake in a basin of water in a 150C oven for about 1 hour.

Optional: Sprinkle with nutmeg prior to baking.

Bananas in Mars

Serves 4. A recipe from the inventive 'Spud' Moore
"Great when camping" were his words.

- *4 firm bananas*
- *2 mars bars*

Cut a slice in the banana skin half way down its middle. Slice up mars bars and poke into the slit. Wrap in foil and place in oven or on the BBQ and cook for approximately 3 - 5 minutes. Remove and turn out onto a plate.

Optional: This is really delicious served with a little pouring cream.

Blancmange

Serves 4. A recipe from Jocelyn Wilson.

- *410ml evaporated milk*
- *1 punnet chopped strawberries (or fruit of choice)*
- *2 tbs. honey*
- *1 sachet of gelatine*

Mix milk, fruit and honey together. Dissolve the gelatine in 3 tbs. of boiling water and add to the mixture, stirring well. Pour into individual bowls. Allow to set in the fridge for a couple of hours.

Optional: Substitute 1 cup of fruit with 1 cup of chocolate topping for a change.

Chocolate Balls

A recipe by Grandma Jennette and loved by Matthew, Brady & Harry McCosker.

- *200g sweet digestive biscuits, crushed*
- *3 tbs. cocoa*
- *¾ tin condensed milk*
- *½ cup (60g) desiccated coconut*

Mix crushed biscuit, cocoa and condensed milk together to make a sticky consistency (add more biscuits if required). Using a generous tsp. of mixture, roll into balls and cover in coconut. Chill before serving.

Tip: These can also be frozen.

Chocolate Bananas

Makes 6

- *¾ cup (185m) milk chocolate*
- *3 bananas*

Melt chocolate in microwave, check every 20 seconds and stir. Remove skin and slice bananas in half. Roll in melted chocolate and place on a tray for cooling. Chill before serving.

Optional: Substitute bananas for strawberries, melons, slices of orange or whtever fruit is in season.

Chocolate Dipped Fruit

Serves 4

- *200g milk chocolate*
- *2 bananas, thickly sliced*
- *1 punnet strawberries, washed and hulled*
- *¾ cup (125g) dried apricots*

Line baking tray with baking paper. Place chocolate in microwave-safe bowl and cook on high, stirring every 20 seconds, until melted. Using your hand, dip fruit, one piece at a time, into chocolate to coat about ¾ of each piece of fruit. Place fruit in single layer on baking tray, refrigerate until set.

Chocolate Nut Clusters

Makes 24

- *¼ cup (55g) shelled, unsalted pistachios*
- *¼ cup (55g) slivered almonds*
- *200g dark chocolate*
- *½ cup (85g) sultanas*

Line baking tray with baking paper. Heat small heavy base frying pan, toast pistachios and almonds, stirring constantly, until browned lightly (take care not to scorch nuts because they burn easily). Remove nuts from hot pan. Place chocolate in microwave-safe bowl and cook on high, stirring every 20 seconds, until melted. Stir nuts and sultanas into chocolate. Use a heaped tablespoon to drop chocolate mixture onto prepared tray. Refrigerate, uncovered, until set.

Crunchy Banana on a Stick

Serves 2 and are nutritious *and* delicious!!

- *1 banana, cut lengthways in half*
- *2 skewers*
- *½ tub organic banana or vanilla yoghurt*
- *½ cup (60g) of crushed crunchie cookies
  (any will do, as long as they're crunchy)*

Thread each banana half onto a skewer. Spread with some yoghurt and roll in cookie crumbs.

Cyndi's Real Custard

Serves 4 - 6. Recipe from Cyndi O'Meara.

- *3 organic free-range eggs, beaten*
- *2 cups organic milk*
- *¼ cup (55g) organic sugar*
- *1 tsp. vanilla essence*

Combine eggs, milk and sugar in a saucepan, stir over medium heat (not too hot or custard will separate) until it coats the back of a metal spoon. Transfer immediately into a glass bowl standing in cold water. Add vanilla, stirring occasionally, while it cools.

Egg Custard

Makes 2 cups. Kim's Mum Jennette used to make this with prune snow, delicious!

- *500ml milk*
- *5 tbs. caster sugar*
- *2 egg yolks*
- *2 tbs. cornflour*

Bring the milk and 2 tbs. sugar to boil in a saucepan over a medium heat. Whisk the yolks and remaining sugar together, then gradually fold in the cornflour to form a pale yellow paste. Carefully pour ½ of the boiled milk into the yolk mixture, whisking to incorporate. Return the remaining milk to the heat and bring to the boil, quickly whisk in the yolk mixture. Continue mixing until it returns to the boil. Transfer to a clean, dry bowl and cover the surface with cling wrap. Chill until required. To use the custard once it has been chilled, beat until smooth. An electric beater gives a much smoother result than beating by hand.

Fluffy Pudding

Serves 4. A recipe from Gwen Colyer ... *Sooo* easy!!

- *1 pkt jelly*
- *375ml can evaporated milk*

Dissolve jelly in 1 cup boiling water, cool and add cold evaporated milk, beat until frothy. Place in the fridge until set.

Optional: Serve with whatever fruit compliments the flavour of the jelly.

Frozen Fruit Treats

Serves 4 - 6

- *1 punnet strawberries, washed and hulled*
- *2 thick slices of pineapple, chopped*
- *2 bananas*
- *250ml orange or apple juice*

Combine all ingredients into a blender and process, till smooth. Pour into an ice block mould with paddle sticks or small paper cups and freeze. Serve partially defrosted, with a spoon if in a cup, or fully frozen if in a stick mould.

Fried Banana with Ice-Cream

Serves 2

- *2 ripe bananas*
- *2 tbs. butter*
- *1 tbs. brown sugar*
- *2 scoops vanilla ice-cream*

Preheat heavy frying pan, melt butter. Add bananas and sprinkle with sugar. Cook for 1 minute, turn and cook for a further minute, or until they reach desired doneness. Serve each with a scoop of ice-cream.

Fruit Kebabs

Serves 4 - 6. Recipe from Jen Whittington.

- *1 packet skewers*
- *Choice of 2 fruits (berries, melon, citrus (whatever you have in the fridge or in the fruit basket)*
- *Choice of fruit yoghurt or 1 tbs. of organic honey*

Dice fruit into bite-size pieces (skin and clean, where required). Thread the chosen fruits alternatively onto a skewer, leaving enough room at the base so the skewer can be held. Drizzle with yoghurt or honey.

Homemade LCM'S

Makes 8

- *2½ cups (200g) of rice bubbles*
- *½ cup of 100's & 1000's*
- *1½ cups of marshmallows*
- *4 tbs. butter, melted, plus a little extra for greasing*

Mix rice bubbles, 100's and 1000's and 1 cup chopped marshmallows in a bowl. Melt remaining marshmallows, add butter and mix, then pour over ingredients combining well. Pour into a greased tray and pat down. Place in fridge to set ... Remove, cut and serve! *Yummy!!*

Honey Joys

A favourite in all kid's lunch boxes!

- *3 tbs. butter*
- *⅓ cup (75g) sugar*
- *1 tbs. honey*
- *4 cups (320g) cornflakes*

Preheat oven 150C. Heat butter, sugar and honey in small saucepan till frothy then remove from heat. Add cornflakes and mix well. Spoon into patty cake cases and bake for 10 minutes.

Jelly Snow

Serves 4.

- *1 pkt jelly (any flavour)*
- *1 cup (125g) frozen berries, partially thawed*
- *2 cups vanilla ice-cream*

Make up a packet of jelly and leave until almost set. Blend with a hand held mixer or blender, it goes frothy and pale. Leave to set completely. Serve with purple ice cream - made by mixing berries through ice-cream.

Livened Ice-Cream

A recipe from Robyn Smith, Geraldton WA.

- *1 pkt jelly (any flavour)*
- *Vanilla ice-cream*

Robyn says "To 'liven' up ice-cream, sprinkle jelly crystals over the top. There are lots of flavours and colours, and a little goes a long way!"

Mars Bar Slice

Serves 6

- *3 mars bars*
- *4 tbs. butter, plus a little extra for greasing*
- *4 cups (320g) rice bubbles*

In a microwave proof dish, melt mars bars and butter for a couple of minutes. Add rice bubbles and mix well. Press into lightly greased tray. Refrigerate and cut into slices when ready to serve.

Marshmallow Medley

Serves 4. Another little treasure from Aine Watkins.

- *12 marshmallows*
- *¼ cup (80g) sour cream*
- *4 mandarins*
- *1½ tbs. shredded coconut*

Mix all together with a spoon, chill and serve.

Mini-Muffins

Makes 12. You will be surprised how quick and easy these are.

- *1 cup (175g) self raising flour*
- *250ml cream, not whipped*
- *3 tbs. brown sugar*

Combine all ingredients and mix well. Pour into greased mini-muffin tray. Bake 10 minutes at 180C or until golden brown.

Optional: Add ½ punnet of fresh blueberries or raspberries, or whatever fourth ingredient you like.

Rice Pudding

Serves 4. A recipe from the beautiful Mary Moore.

- *1 litre milk*
- *½ cup (55g) rice*
- *2 tbs. sugar*
- *½ tsp. vanilla essence*

Preheat oven. Add all ingredients to a baking dish place in the middle of a 150C oven and bake for 1½ hours.

Popcorn Parcels

Makes 6

- *3 cups (120g) coloured popcorn*
- *200g white chocolate*
- *½ liquorice strap, cut into long, thin strips*

Melt chocolate in the microwave until soft, check every 20 seconds and stir, add popcorn. Stir gently until well combined. Divide into six equal portions, shaping into a ball. Place on a tray and insert liquorice. Chill until firm.

Prune Snow

Serves 4 and is remembered as a favourite of Kim's from her childhood!

- *1 cup (150g) prunes*
- *2 tbs. caster sugar*
- *2 eggwhites*

Place prunes into a saucepan and cover with water. Cook for approximately 10 minutes, or until soft. Remove from heat and allow to cool. Meanwhile, beat eggwhites until fluffy, add sugar, bit by bit, and continue to beat, until stiff. Remove seeds from prunes, and mash. Fold eggwhites into prunes and serve with custard.

Optional: You can use your egg yolks to make a delicious egg custard.

Sesame & Honey Bars

Makes 12. This is made in a couple of minutes and is really tasty.

- *1 cup (100g) sesame seeds*
- *1 cup (100g) rolled oats*
- *½ cup (160g) manuka honey (or organic honey)*
- *½ cup (115g) butter, plus extra for greasing*

Preheat oven to 180C. Grind sesame seeds and rolled oats together in a food processor. Melt honey and butter in a small saucepan. Add salt and then pour mixture into the food processor. Blend and turn out into a well-buttered baking tray (can line with baking paper instead of greasing the tray). Bake for 20 - 25 minutes, or until golden brown. Cut the biscuits in the tin and then leave them to cool.

Summer Yoghurt Treat

Serves 1

- *½ cup (50g) toasted fruit muesli*
- *2 tbs. organic yoghurt of choice*
- *1 tbs. of mixed fruit (or fruit of choice, i.e. strawberries, banana, melon, grapes, blueberries, raspberries)*

Place muesli in a glass or bowl. Top with yoghurt and sprinkle with mixed fruit.

Sweet Carrot Snacks

Serves 2 - 4

- *4 chilled carrots*
- *2 tbs. manuka honey*
- *1 tsp. sesame seeds*

Peel chilled carrots, cut length by half, then slice into four. Add honey and sesame seeds to small side bowl. Great for after school. You can also use organic tahini as a substitute for honey. A nutritious and healthy snack.

Sweet Toasted Sandwich

Serves 4.   A great idea from Meredith Mullaly.

- *8 pieces of fruit bread*
- *400g tin of apples*
- *1 tsp. cinnamon sugar*
- *1 tbs. butter*

Butter bread and turn upside down. Thickly coat 4 slices with apple and sprinkle with cinnamon sugar. Place remaining slices of buttered fruit bread, butter side up, on mixture. Toast as you would a normal toasted sandwich.

Optional: Serve plain or with ice-cream.

Toffees

Makes 12

- 2 cups sugar
- 1 cup (250ml) water
- 1 tbs. vinegar
- 100's & 1,000's

Combine sugar, water and vinegar in a saucepan. Stir over medium heat until sugar has completely dissolved. Bring to the boil, reduce heat slightly. Boil without stirring for 20 minutes (it is ready when a drop of the mixture in cold water hardens). Pour into little patty cases and decorate with hundreds and thousands. Leave to set at room temperature.

Yummy Kebabs

Makes 6

- 1 punnet of strawberries, washed and hulled
- 2 kiwi fruit
- 3 bananas
- Assorted lollies

Cut kiwi fruit and banana into chunks. Thread them, plus strawberries and lollies onto bamboo skewers. Remove sharp ends before serving to children.

For The Lunch Box

Anyone who thinks the art of conversation is dead ought to tell a child to go to bed!

Robert Gallagher

A healthy school lunch box is something we Mummies try to aim for everyday. The best lunch is one that's nutritious and quick to prepare, but also fun and easy to eat. Encouraging your children to be involved in choosing foods and preparing their lunch can help ensure that it not only gets eaten, but enjoyed as well.

Fresh Fruit

With the price rises of food in general of late it makes working on a tight weekly shop very hard! However, if you shop wisely, you can still afford these and many more fresh fruit and vegetable ideas for the lunch boxes.

Our suggestion ... MARKETS!!! Locate your nearest markets and shop there. Not only are the prices of fresh fruit and vegetables MUCH CHEAPER they are usually home grown, organic, vine-ripened and TASTE SENSATIONAL!!

- *Apples: Ask the vendor which are the crunchy varieties at time of purchase as NO-ONE, least of all a child, likes a floury apple! The skin of an apple is the best nutrients wise.*
- *Apricot*
- *Bananas*
- *Blueberries*
- *Chunks of pineapple*
- *Cubes of watermelon, honey dew or rockmelon*
- *Grapes – white or black*
  (the skin of the black is FULL of great anti-oxidants!!)
- *Kiwi fruit*
- *Mango (buy plenty in season and freeze for out of season)*

---

4 Ingredients

- *Mandarins*
- *Nashi – crunchy and juicy, our children love these*
- *Nectarine*
- *Oranges – quartered*
- *Passionfruit, cut in half*
- *Peach*
- *Pear*
- *Plum*
- *Raspberries*
- *Strawberries*

Vegetable Sticks

- *Carrot sticks*
- *Celery sticks*
- *Cherry tomatoes*
- *Lebanese cucumbers, cut into strips*
- *Peas in the pod*
- *Strips of yellow, red or green peppers*
- *Whole green beans*

Dairy

You read everywhere that experts suggest you include one serve of dairy food in a lunch box every day. One serve is equal to:

- *250ml of milk. In the summer, try freezing milk overnight and wrap in a cloth for the lunch box to minimize the sweating - by lunchtime it will be ready to drink.*
- *Cheese slices, cubes or sticks*
- *Yoghurt - natural or fruit yoghurt. Try freezing a tub of yoghurt and placing in the lunch box. As with the milk – by lunchtime, it will have partially thawed and be ready to eat.*

Protein Food

Choose one or more of these protein rich foods as a starter for your sandwich:

- *Baked beans (choose low salt where available; consider trying Mexican, barbeque, curried flavours)*
- *Bean salad*
- *3 bean mix*
- *Canned fish, such as sardines, mackerel*
- *Cheese*
- *Egg (hard boiled, lightly curried)*
- *Falafel*
- *Fish patties*
- *Lentil patties*
- *Peanut butter*
- *Plain unsalted nuts*
- *Sliced cold meats such as ham, turkey, smoked salmon, chicken, lamb, corned beef, roast beef, ham,*
- *Cold sliced meatloaf or meatballs*
- *Tuna in brine or salmon. Try the mini cans of tuna with added flavours, such as tuna and sun-dried tomatoes or tuna and lemon.*

A More Exciting Sandwich

1. *Triple Deckers – this is really easy and fun. Make a sandwich with 3 slices of bread and two layers of filling. Remove the crusts and cut into three strips.*
2. *Pita Pockets – half a pocket bread filled with your choice of filling, e.g. lean meat, salad, egg, grated cheese, carrot, etc.*
3. *As above, use a variety of different breads.*
4. *Pack sandwich fillings separately so that children can make their own sandwiches to avoid, "They're too soggy!!"*
5. *Buy different cutting shapes for your toddlers (use the excess for breadcrumbs to avoid waste) but it is fun for them to eat a shark shaped sandwich!!*

Sandwiches

Try to include lots of varieties of bread, fillings and spreads to retain interest in sandwiches.   There are many breads and breadrolls to choose from. Wholemeal, multigrain, rye, corn, flat, pita, sourdough, pumpernickel, mountain, lavash, white fibre-enriched, omega 3 enriched, soy and linseed, herb ... The list goes on and on!

- *Bagels*
- *Corn thins*
- *Crackers*
- *Crispbreads*
- *Crumpets*
- *English muffins*
- *Foccacias*
- *Fruit loaf/buns*
- *Mountain bread - try wheat, corn, rice or barley*
- *Pasta and rice: make a salad with Italian dressing, chunks of cheese and lots of raw vegetables*
- *Pikelets*
- *Pita pocket bread*
- *Rice: try our easy fried rice recipe and add lots of steamed vegetables*
- *Rice cakes*
- *Scones*

Super Sandwich Ideas

Gathered from some Super Mummies in our lives!

1. Roast beef, tomato, grainy mustard and shredded iceberg lettuce
2. Peanut butter and mashed banana
3. Cheese, marmite and a sprinkling of finely chopped onion
4. Peanut butter and bean sprouts (sounds unusual but is really tasty!!)
5. Banana on raisin bread
6. Cheese with grated carrot, lettuce and sultanas
7. Tuna and tomato
8. Baked beans on a bread roll
9. hicken, chopped celery and walnuts and a dash of mayo to combine
10. Cottage cheese mixed with chopped apple and dates (yummo!)
11. Ham, chutney, lettuce and grated carrot and cheese on a foccacia
12. Egg and lettuce
13. Apple and cream cheese
14. Salmon mixed with cream cheese to bind
15. Cheese and tomato
16. Ham and cheese
17. Cream cheese, chopped celery and sultanas
18. Peanut butter and grated carrot
19. Leftover roast meat with grated carrot, chopped lettuce and chutney
20. Tuna, lettuce and tomato sauce
21. Ham, cheese and a pineapple ring (make sure it is dry before placing on the sandwich)
22. Mashed banana
23. Grated carrot, cheese and mayonnaise
24. Curried egg
25. Bacon, lettuce and tomato
26. Banana and sultanas

Nut Butter Sandwiches

Makes 1

- *100g of chopped nuts (choose from cashews, almonds, macadamia, walnuts or peanuts)*
- *2 tbs. sultanas (or raisins)*
- *1 tsp. walnut oil*
- *2 slices wholemeal bread, per person*

Blend the nuts and sultanas together in a food processor to make a smooth, thick paste (this takes some time). Add the oil to get the right consistency for your spread. Spread one side of the bread with the nut butter and place the other slice of bread over the top and cut into four. Serve.

Note: Extra nut spread can be kept in the fridge for up to one week in a sealed jar.

Dried Fruit

Banana Chips

- *4 bananas*

Peel and slice banana thinly. Bake in a hot oven 220C for
15 - 20 minutes, or until crisp.

Banana Coated Chips

- *The above banana chips*
- *120g milk chocolate, melted*

Dip the banana chips into the melted chocolate and place onto a
baking paper lined tray. Pop into the fridge to set before serving.

Optional: Works just as nicely with other dried fruit.

Others

You can purchase a really wide variety of dried fruits from
supermarkets and health food stores.

Or, if you are like Errol McCosker (Kim's Dad), dry them with your
own dehydrator ... His dried mango is simply divine and his
grandchildren love it!

Make Eating Food Healthy Again
It's not that hard!

Food is the cheapest form of entertainment. When I was traveling and backpacking around Europe in my late teens I couldn't afford to do too much except enjoy the countryside, walk through the city streets and hike the beautiful mountains. But what I could afford to do was enjoy food and conversation with a group of friends.

The fact that this recipe book is made up of recipes with just 4 ingredients makes it a very easy, cheap way to have fun. Food surrounds everything we do; from the minute we wake up till we go to bed we punctuate our life around our meals and snacks. So why not make it easy and healthy at the same time with this refreshing, extraordinary recipe book.

When I want to, or have to make a meal, I often spend some time looking for a recipe, the reason being as many recipes which have lots of ingredients I usually find I am missing one or more ingredients, so I have to keep looking until I find a recipe with all the ingredients. With this recipe book you will always have the ingredients; the guide of what you should stock your pantry with will help.

If you are going to make the effort to make food, why not make it healthy! Most foods whether it is chocolate cake, lemon butter or custard can be healthy, it all depends on the ingredients you use. So buy good quality ingredients and all the recipes in this book will be healthy. But what is good quality? What is healthy? The media and science has confused the masses, most of us throw up our hands in despair and decide to just eat what we want. So I'm going to make it easy. "Nature makes all the healthy foods and everything else is junk."

Ask yourself the following; who makes margarine, artificial sweeteners, additives, modified milks and the like? So when you are choosing the ingredients for your recipes make sure they are the best, choose butter, organic eggs, organic unbleached flour, rapadura sugar (instead of white sugar), real mayonnaise, pastry made with butter, cold pressed oils fresh fruit and vegetables and the like.

The rule is 80/20, for 80% of the time eat good wholesome foods, but remember to have fun and enjoy the other side as well, but just 20%.

Congratulations Rachael and Kim, what a fabulous book for busy Mum's and Dad's as well as a great book for all ages, from the teenage years to the older generation. Everyone will reap the benefits of this fabulous 4 ingredient cookbook.

Cyndi O'Meara

Nutritionist, Presenter and Author of
Changing Habits Changing Lives.

A recipe for all Mothers

Today I left some dishes dirty;
The bed I made at 3:30
The nappies soaked a little longer,
The odour grew a little stronger.
The crumbs I spilt the day before
Are staring at me from the floor.
The fingerprints, there on the wall
Will likely still be there, next fall.
The dirty streaks on the window panes
Will still be there next time it rains.
"Shame on you old lazy-bones," I say
"And just what have you done, today?"

I nursed a baby till he slept,
I held a toddler while he wept.
I played a game of hide and seek
I squeezed a toy, so it would squeak.
I pulled a wagon, sang a song,
Taught a child right from wrong.
What did I do this whole day through?
Not much that shows, I guess it's true...
Unless you think that what I've done
Might be important to someone
With bright blue eyes and soft blonde hair
If that is true, I've done my share.

Joanne Green

Drinks

Apple, Carrot & Ginger Juice

A great breakfast drink!

- *2 granny smith apples*
- *2 carrots*
- *1 tbs. fresh ginger*

Blend or juice, don't peel, as most of the vitamins are found just beneath the skin.

Apple, Celery & Carrot Juice

- *2 granny smith apples*
- *2 celery sticks (it's best to remove the strings)*
- *2 carrots*

Blend or juice.

Banana & Maple Supreme

- *½ cup (125ml) chilled milk*
- *1 ripe banana*
- *2 tsp. maple syrup*

Blend altogether. Pour into a large glass and decorate with a slice of banana.

Banana Lassi

Makes 2

- *1 large ripe banana*
- *250g natural yoghurt*
- *½ cup (125ml) milk*
- *1 tbs. raw sugar (if needed)*

Place all ingredients in a food processor and blend until smooth.

Energiser Drink

- *1 ripe banana*
- *½ cup (110g) fresh or frozen berries*
  (strawberries or raspberries or mixed berries)
- *½ cup (125ml) skim milk*
- *¼ cup (62ml) low-fat natural yoghurt*

Combine all ingredients in a blender and blend until smooth. Add ½ cup of ice for a frappe effect. Serve in a tall glass.

Grape Melon Drink

- ¼ watermelon
- 1 bunch of grapes, without stalk

Blend or juice.

Homemade Lemonade

- 1 cup (125g) caster sugar
- 1 cup (250ml) lemon juice
- 3 cups (750ml) soda water, chilled

Place the caster sugar in a saucepan with 1 cup water and stir over low heat until the sugar dissolves. Allow to cool. Stir in the lemon juice. To serve, top with chilled soda water and lots of crushed ice.

Melon Delight

- ¾ cup (185ml) pineapple juice
- 4 slices honeydew melon
- 1 tsp. honey

Blend the ingredients with ½ a cup of ice and pour into a large glass.

Minty Apple Iced Tea

- *3 peppermint tea bags*
- *500ml apple juice*
- *8 mint leaves, torn*
- *1 small crunch apple, thinly sliced*

Soak teabags in 2 cups boiling water and stand for 10 minutes. Discard bags. Pour tea into a jug, mix in juice and mint. Cover with food wrap and chill for an hour before serving in tall glasses over plenty of ice. Add apple slices, stir and serve.

Orange, Lemon & Strawberry Juice

- *2 oranges*
- *1 lemon*
- *1 punnet strawberries*

Peel oranges and lemon and quarter, add strawberries and blend. This is a great *'fresh start'* juice.

Orange Yoghurt Shake

- *2 large oranges*
- *200g natural Greek yoghurt*
- *1 tsp. honey*

Peel oranges and place in a blender with yoghurt and honey.

Peanut, Pine & Banana Shake

- *500g organic yoghurt*
- *2 chilled bananas*
- *2 cups chilled organic pineapple pieces or fresh pineapple*
- *½ cup (150g) smooth organic peanut butter*

Combine all ingredients in a blender and process till smooth.

Pina Colada Shake

Recipe from Cyndi O'Meara.

- *1 pineapple, juiced*
- *1 cup (250ml) coconut milk*
- *2 bananas*
- *1 cup ice*

Combine all ingredients in a blender and process till smooth.
Serve chilled.

Pineapple & Mint Juice

- *1 pineapple, peeled and chopped*
- *5 sprigs fresh mint leaves*

Blend well and serve chilled over crushed ice.

Strawberry Smoothie

- *1 cup (250ml) chilled organic apple juice (if more than 90% juice, or 4 apples)*
- *2 ripe bananas*
- *1 tbs. flaxseed oil*
- *1 punnet chilled strawberries, washed and hulled*

Blend all ingredients together and serve chilled ... YUM!

Great Combination Meals

As suggested by Rachael's brother 'Spud'
a Chef with over 20 years experience.

Beef

1. Beef Wellington, beef stock & red wine reduction,
    beans, garlic and pine nuts
2. Pesto stuffed steak, mushroom risotto, rocket,
    oven-roasted tomato
3. Quick meatloaf, mixed green salad, balsamic
    and garlic dressing
4. Roast Beef, seasoned roast vegetables, gravy, damper

Chicken

1. Chicken, pumpkin and chickpea curry, fluffy rice,
    yoghurt and pappadums
2. Cheese and prosciutto chicken, sweet potato and baby spinach
3. Cajun chicken kebab, spinach and strawberry salad,
    chilli mayonnaise
4. Mascarpone and coriander chicken, garlic potato and
    green salad with balsamic and garlic dressing.

Fish

1. Baked salmon with pesto crust, polenta, English spinach,
    shaved parmesan & marinated olives
2. Herb baked barramundi, sautéed lemon potato, asparagus
    & balsamic dressing
3. Moroccan salmon, antipasto tart, hummus, rocket lettuce
4. Pasta with crab and lemon cream, green salad, vinaigrette,
    garlic bread

Lamb

1. Lamb shank casserole, mash potato with pine nuts, seasoned roast vegetables
2. Asian lamb cutlets, onion jam, Queensland beer battered vegetables, coriander
3. Tandoori lamb cutlets, Greek yoghurt and egg mayonnaise, avocado salsa
4. Lamb and bacon parcels, spring salad, balsamic and garlic dressing

Pork

1. Chinese BBQ pork, soba noodles & easy Thai dressing
2. Pork & bacon wrap, brie bruschetta, olive oil, fresh basil
3. Pork tenderloin with mustard sauce, rosemary and thyme potato, asparagus butter & parmesan
4. Roast pork, grilled pears, roasted corn, parmesan & cayenne, gravy

Vegetarian

1. Sour cream quiche, green salad with Greek yoghurt and egg mayonnaise dressing
2. Green bean curry, fluffy rice, yoghurt, pappadums
3. Pasta with tomato and basil, brie bruschetta (with or without tomatoes)
4. Mushroom risotto, shaved parmesan, roasted tomato, rocket and asparagus.

Handy Home Tips

Interesting Tips for the Household

This book has 'morphed' into what it has ultimately become. When you start to tell people what you are working on they come up with some fabulous suggestions. One such suggestion was to include a 'Handy Home Tips' section.

Here follows some of those terrific little tips, gathered from some of our nearest and dearest.

Alleviate discomfort when plucking your eyebrows: By smoothing baby teething gel over the area to numb the pain.

Bandaids: Removing is easy if you soak a piece of cotton wool in baby oil and rub over the tape.

Blender: Cleaning your blender is much quicker if you fill it about a third with hot water and add a couple of drops of your washing detergent, then turn it on!

Boiling Pasta: Add at least 4-5 cups of water to a large pot. One tablespoon of salt should be added to the water as it begins to boil. If the salt is added too soon it can give off an odour, which can affect the taste of the pasta. If it is added immediately before the pasta, the salt may not have enough time to completely dissolve in the water. The salt helps bring out the flavour in the pasta and helps it hold its shape.

Brittle & flaking fingernails: Mix 2 level teaspoons of gelatine into 1/2 glass of fruit juice or cold water. Drink at once and repeat daily for at least 6 weeks. You should see a dramatic improvement in your nails after about 2 months.

Brittle nails: To avoid, massage cod liver oil, which is rich in vitamin A, into cuticles and nails. After three months, nails will be stronger and cuticles smoother.

Broken Glass: Use a piece of bread to pick up the fragments of broken glass.

Brunette or red hair: To add shine, after shampooing rinse with fresh brewed black coffee which you have cooled, followed by cold water.

Carry a water bottle with you at all times: Water flushes toxins in the body, as well as filling you up.

Celery: Stop celery wilting by wrapping it in alfoil, when putting in the refrigerator, and it will keep for weeks.

Chewing gum in children's hair: Dab with a cloth soaked with eucalyptus oil, gum should come out without tears.

Cockroaches: To repel, mix equal parts of borax and sugar and place where cockroaches frequent, e.g. under fridge and dishwashers.

Disinfectant: Teatree oil, added to cleaners or in the rinsing water, is a natural disinfectant.

Drains of your sink: To clean, put a tbs. of bicarbonate of soda down the sink followed by two tbs. of vinegar, and let stand.

Eyes: Relax your eyes at regular intervals when reading or using a computer by taking regular 5 minute breaks, or focusing at a distance of 5 metres away.

Fabric interior of your car: To remove marks from, use home brand baby wipes; even the long-term stains will come off ... these really do work!

Fish: To cook fish, it generally takes 10 minutes to cook, per inch of thickness. Just to be sure it doesn't overcook, start checking the fish at 7-8 minutes.

Flowers: Cutting an inch off the bottom of the stems and placing into water within 13 seconds (prevents inhalation of air) and adding a little bleach in the water will keep your flowers longer, because the water is cleaner. Change water regularly.

Fridges and freezers: To keep smelling fresh, sprinkle a few drops of vanilla essence onto a damp cloth and wipe the interior walls and shelves. To dispel odours, place a small container of bicarbonate of soda inside the fridge.

For an instant facelift: Beat an eggwhite and apply it to your skin. Leave on for about 10 minutes and rinse off. Your skin will be tighter and appear firmer.

For puffy eyes: Soak two tea bags, then place them in the freezer for a few minutes; place on eyes & lay back & relax! Or, grate a raw potato, mould it into a mushy pack, and put it on your eyes and lids for 10-20 minutes. The potato starch will help smooth eye-area skin and ease away puffiness.

Green hair: Remove the green tinge from your hair, as a result of swimming in chlorinated water, by washing your hair in 5 aspirin tablets dissolved in a third cup of shampoo. Or alternatively, 3 tbs. of vinegar in your shampoo.

Housework: Hire help, or barter for help. If you can't afford a weekly cleaner, employ someone to do the hard work once a fortnight – work this into your budget; it is worth every cent of the exhilarating feeling that walking into a clean house offers!!

Iceberg lettuce: Lasts much longer if wrapped in alfoil before placing it in the vegetable tray in the fridge. And it's especially good during winter when you don't use lettuce much.

Iron: To clean the underneath, wipe it with a cloth soaked in cold tea. This will remove stains immediately.

Leather lounge suite: To clean, wash it with warm, soapy water using a nail brush and cloth. Allow to dry then smother the cleaned area with Vaseline; rub it in with a cloth to get the residue off. This works better than most expensive cleaners.

Leather Lounge: To revive, polish it with linseed oil and vinegar, in portions of 1:2.

Lower back pain: To relieve, sleep with a pillow under your knees to take the pressure off your lower back and have a good nights sleep.

Make-do hair spray: Getting ready for a big night out and realise you're out of hair spray? Try dissolving a tablespoon of sugar in a glass of hot water, wait till it cools and then put into a spray bottle. It's effective and environmentally friendly, too!

Mascara : As it gets older and starts to dry up, soak in a mug of hot water before use.

Meat: Remove from fridge about an hour before BBQ'ing. Your meat will be more succulent as a result.

Minimise redness of spots on your face: By soaking a piece of cotton wool in eye drops and holding on spot for 20 seconds.

Moths: Repel pantry moths by keeping an open packet of epsom salts on the shelf.

Nail polish: Will last longer if you keep it in the fridge.

Nice smelling car: Place a tube of fabric softener concentrate under the seats (do not pierce; apple and lavender particularly nice). The diversity and staying power of the scents are great and they work better than expensive car deodorisers.

Nicotine stains on fingers: Can be removed by rubbing with nail polish remover or by simply giving up smoking!!

Oven: Reduce the unpleasant smell left from oven cleaners by baking some citrus peelings on a low heat.

Oven Cleaning: To reduce, line the bottom of your oven with aluminium foil cut to size. The foil catches drips and grease, and can be easily replaced when dirty.

Pearls: To clean your pearls, shake in a bag of uncooked rice.

Razor burn: Avoid razor burn after shaving your legs by moisturising beforehand. While shaving cream is the most popular method, try prepping your leg with hair conditioner for a few minutes before shaving. It will hold moisture on the leg longer and provide a very smooth shave.

Remove baked-on stains from glass baking dishes: By soaking in a strong solution of borax and water.

Removing mascara: A cheaper and just as effective way to do this is to use baby oil. Simply dip a cotton bud in, or cover some cotton wool with, baby oil and gently wipe over your lashes. The oil will also soften the skin around your eyes, so there is no need for eye creams, either.

Revitalising eye gel: Keep your eye gel in the fridge to really soothe tired eyes or cool you down on a hot day.

School lunches: Make more fun by using a cookie cutter to cut sandwiches into shapes!

Self-raising flour: To make, mix 2 kg plain flour, 2 tbs. bicarbonate of soda and ¼ cup cream of tartar. Sift well.

Sharp lip-line and eye-line: Put your eye-liner or lip-liner pencil in the freezer, briefly, before sharpening, to get a fine point.

Spaghetti: When cooking, add a tsp. of cooking oil or a tsp. of butter to the water in rice, noodles or spaghetti. This will prevent the water from boiling over and strands from sticking together.

Stainless steel sink: To brighten, use a damp cloth soaked in vinegar.

Steak:

Cook steak in a pan as follows:

1. Oil the steaks, not the pan, using extra virgin olive oil.
2. Set heat on medium.
   Always have the pan hot before starting.
3. Place steaks in pan; do not turn until sealed and juices have risen (usually 1 to 1 ½ minutes).
   Turn and continue to cook to desired state.

Cooking Times (depending on thickness):

Rare: 2-5 minutes
Medium: 8-12 minutes
Well: 12-15 minutes

Strawberries: Purchase strawberries red all-over. The redder near the hull of the fruit the sweeter.

Stuck-on food in pots, pans, and casserole dishes: Fill the pan with water and place a fabric softener sheet in the water. Allow the pan to soak overnight. The food will wipe right out!

Swollen hands: If you have a ring stuck on your finger, due to your fingers swelling, soak your hand in ice water till the ring slips off.

Take the generic brand on prescriptions: They often come from the same company and are exactly the same as the full-priced version.

Tie a small bell to any door: leading out of the house and you'll be able to hear a small child making their escape!

Timber floors: which have been sealed can be cleaned with cold tea on a mop. A little vinegar in the bucket of water with the detergent helps to remove any grease from kitchen floors.

Try using some cold cucumber slices: ... on your eyes at the end of the night to relieve tired eyes. An oldie, but a goodie.

Washing Clothes: Hang clothes as soon as you can after washing, to reduce creasing.

When giving distasteful medicine to young children: First, run an ice cube over their tongue; this temporarily freezes the taste buds.

When starting a new fitness regime: Don't over commit yourself, as you will soon lose interest; start with a little activity and increase as your fitness level does.

When travelling with a baby: Take some bicarbonate of soda with you in a small zip-lock bag. Should your baby be sick, simply sprinkle clothes with the soda. Brush off when dry and odour will have disappeared.

Whiten your fingernail tips: ... by soaking your nails in lemon juice.

Biographies
Rachael Bermingham

Rachael Bermingham (nee Moore) was born in Stanthorpe before moving to the Sunshine Coast at 11 where she grew up & still resides with husband Paul (a renovator) & gorgeous son Jaxson 3. She is also 'wicked' step mum to Lee 19 & Teri 17.

Working from her home office, Rachael co-runs 4 Ingredients & Sunshine Coast Speakers & solo operates her personal speaking engagements & Read My Lips: her 1st self published book she co-wrote to inspire women to achieve their goals (first published 14/2/06) which she penned out while feeding baby Jaxson.

A born entrepreneur Rachael showed her keen eye for business early on with the launch of her first business venture (the first mobile hair salon on the Sunshine Coast) at age 19 that she built up for a year, & sold for a profit before going onto experience a host of bold careers to satisfy her adventurous nature, including diving & shark feeding at Underwater World before her passion for business returned in the form of travel.

After a 5 year stint as a Flight Centre travel agent, Rachael entered into what could have been considered a fatal business move by opening her own travel agency just 3 months prior to September 11. This experience would ultimately prove to be a pivotal point in her career igniting the development of an ability which would be invaluable for Rachael, Read My Lips & 4 Ingredients & inspire others in business around the world as well.

With the travel trade in a spin, Rachael didn't give up; instead she worked well into the early morning hours teaching herself how to market so her business would survive in the industry's most ruinous era. Researching & testing LOTS & LOTS (& LOTS!) of strategies, she learnt the art of marketing & found she LOVED it & thankfully had a real knack for it.

Her talent for marketing & publicity soon became well known and requests from others to help them also started coming in. She sat on various business boards including an RSL, town developmental board and a business women's board before leaving travel to take on the first of many businesses she would build from a tiny turnover to an astonishing MULTI MILLION dollar turnovers within months AND without spending a cent on advertising! Right up to an hour of going into labour, Rachael was still actively involved in mentoring and helping business owners in 6 different countries.

Within weeks of becoming a Mum, Rachael known for her abundant energy & enthusiasm continued to pursue her passion for business instigating a motivational seminar for women encompassing life, health, wealth and business success strategies with the help of some of girlfriends that ran for 2 years and morphed into the book Read My Lips.

It was by giving Read My Lips to Kim as a gift at Jaxsons 1st birthday party that would prove to be the beginning of yet another incredible journey for Rachael. Prompted by Rachael's passing comment of 'They say everyone has a good book in them' Kim entrusted her own fabulous idea for a book with Rachael (a cookbook using a few ingredients) which Rachael immediately loved and proceeded to prod Kim to start compiling (mainly so Rachael herself could use it!!!) Kim after a few weeks said that she'd do it on the condition 'that you write it with me!'. And the rest is beautiful history!

These days when Rachael's not kicking her heels up and enjoying time with her gorgeous family, she is writing, cooking up a storm with Kim, or speaking at conferences to inspire others to achieve their own goals, how to life balance, time management, how to develop a business from home and of course marketing and publicity.

You can contact Rachael by email; info@4ingredients.com.au Or by snail mail; PO Box 1171 Mooloolaba QLD 4557

Rachael's other business website links;
Read My Lips www.ReadMyLips.com

Speaking bookings www.RachaelBermingham.com

How to write your own book & make it a bestseller
www.HowToWriteYourOwnBook.com.au

Kim McCosker

Kim was born in Stanthorpe and raised there until moving to Mundubbera, Queensland a fantastic little town where many of her wonderful family and friends still live.

Schooled on the Gold Coast, Kim attended Star of the Sea Catholic High School and Griffith University, completing a degree in International Finance in 1998. Kim trained with MLC as a Financial Planner completing her Diploma in Financial Planning through Deakin University in 2000. Kim's natural ease with people, her ability to communicate effortlessly and her home grown country confidence served her extremely well as a successful financial adviser and later as the Queensland State Manager of MLC Private Client Services. After the birth of her second child Kim resigned and decided to contract from home writing financial plans.

It was during this phase of her life that 4 Ingredients was brought into a reality. Kim had the idea, but it was at the insistence of her life long friend Rachael Bermingham that they write the book ... And so over a couple of red wines began the wonderful rollercoaster ride 4 Ingredients would go on to become!

Taking a year to compile and cook, 4 Ingredients (or Kim's fourth child as she lovingly refers to it) was launched on the 14th March, 2007. From an initial print run of 2,000 that was deemed 'over ambitious in a market saturated with cookbooks' Kim and Rachael went on to orchestrate what the trade now refers to simply as "An Absolute Phenomenon!" Not only was 4 ingredients one of the biggest selling titles in both Australia and New Zealand for 2007 but it has just been crowned THE BIGGEST SELLING BOOK in Australia for 2008!

And as Kim will tell you "All because we wanted to save some time and money in the kitchen!"

In addition to this, over the past 8 years Glen and Kim have bought and renovated several properties, including a beautiful 1957 Anglican Church, a beachside shack, and the current property they now live in on the Sunshine Coast's glorious Pelican Waters. Kim maintains the administration, bookwork and finances for their various businesses and financial interests.

Without a sliver of doubt however, the most rewarding of everything accomplished to date has been the birth of her three precious little boys Morgan, 6 Hamilton 3 and Flynn, 6 months old. For Kim, family is *THE MOST IMPORTANT* thing in the world and carries the greatest priority of all she does! Renovations to properties were done with the children playing in the yard, recipes tested with them mixing and stirring, books written around their sleep times and trips made only when her wonderfully supportive and very loved husband Glen could be home for them.

Life presents many opportunities, but having the courage to pursue them, in what is an ever increasingly busy and demanding world, is hard. But Kim is living proof that you can achieve whatever you want in life with exactly that ... Hard work!

You can contact Kim through:
www.4ingredients.com.au or
kim@4ingredients.com.au

Bibliography

Books

Cyndi O'Meara. **Changing Habits Changing Lives.**
Penguin Books Victoria Australia 2000.

Cyndi O'Meara. **Changing Habits Changing Lives Cookbook.**
Penguin Books Victoria Australia 2002.

Donalee Halkett. **Snack it Out.**
Choice Living Po Box 1546, Noosa Heads Queensland Australia 4567.

The Australian Womens Weekly Cookbooks. **Great Vegetarian Food**.
Sydney, Australia. ACP Publishing Pty Ltd, 2001.

Family Circle. **Kids Party Book.** Sydney, Australia.
Murdoch Magazines Pty Ltd, 1995.

Lowery, Barbara. **Quick & Easy Cookbook.** 176 South Creek Road,
Dee Why West, Australia. Summit Books, 1977.

Slater, Nigel. **The 30-Minute Cook**. 27 Wrights Lane, London W8
5TZ, Great Britain. Penguin Group, 1994.

Bjelke- Petersen, Lady Flo. **Classic Country Collection.**
Sydney, Australia. New Holland Publishers, Pty Ltd, 1997.

Concept New Zealand & R & R Kitchens. **Fast Meals.** PO Box 254
Carlton North, Victoria, Australia. R & R Publications Marketing Pty
Ltd, 2005.

Burt, Alison. **Fondue Cookery.** 176 South Creek Road, Dee Why
West, Australia. Summit Books, 1970.

Lloyd Susan. **Dinner Party Cookbook.** 169 Phillip Street, Waterloo,
N.S.W. Australia. Australian Universities Press Pty Ltd, 1974.

Cooking up a storm from the IGA Cauldren Pot. Mundubbera IGA.
Self-published, 2004.

Crofts, Susan. **Susan's Kitchen.** Mundubbera, Queensland. Self-published, 2005.

Webpage

"**Chefs Feed Your Passion.**" 23 December, 2005.
www.chefs.com/recipes

Sydney Markets. "**Healthy Recipes.**" w
ww.betterhealth.vic.gov.au

"**Parentbytes Recipes**." Edition 49.
www.parentbytes.com

Krosch, Renee. "**The Easiest and Tastiest Chicken Recipes Around**." ABC Victoria. 8 May 2006.
www.abc.net.au

Annabella's Kitchen. " **Lamb, Beef & Pork Recipes.**"
www.annabella.net

Larsen, Linda. "**Busy Cooks Recipe Box**" 21 June 2006.
www.busycooks.about.com

Asoliva. "**Spain**."
www.globalgourmet.com

An Australian Government, State and Territory health initiative.
"**Why 2 & 5**." www.gofor2and5.com.au/

"**Easy Meals to Cook**" May 2006.
www.xpress101meal.com/

Jim Rohn.
www.jrohn.com

Index

Invitation

To all who contributed a recipe to this book by way of email, post or phone we would like to extend a *sincere* thank you.

If *YOU* have a fabulous 4 or 5 ingredient recipe and think that others would enjoy cooking it please submit it at: www.4ingredients.co.uk be sure to include name, suburb or town for acknowledgment.

Thank You

Best Wishes & Happy Cooking

KIM & RACHAEL

Kim   Rachael

www.4ingredients.co.uk

Notes